A ROSE IN JUNE

BY

MRS. OLIPHANT

MRS. OLIPHANT

CHAPTER I.

Martha, Martha, thou art careful and troubled about many things. Let the child alone—she will never be young again if she should live a hundred years!"

These words were spoken in the garden of Dinglefield Rectory on a very fine summer day a few years ago. The speaker was Mr. Damerel, the rector, a middle-aged man with very fine, somewhat worn features, a soft benignant smile, and, as everybody said who knew him, the most charming manners in the world. He was a man of very elegant mind as well as manners. He did not preach often, but when he did preach all the educated persons in his congregation felt that they had very choice fare indeed set before them. I am afraid the poor folk liked the curate best, but then the curate liked them best, and it mattered very little to any man or woman of refinement what sentiment existed between the cottagers and the curate. Mr. Damerel was perfectly kind and courteous to everybody, gentle and simple, who came in his way, but he was not fond of poor people in the abstract. He disliked everything that was unlovely, and alas! there are a great many unlovely things in poverty. The rectory garden at Dinglefield is a delightful place. The house is on the summit of a little hill, or rather table-land, for in the front, towards the green, all is level and soft as becomes an English village; but on the other side the descent begins towards the lower country, and from the drawing-room windows and the lawn, where Mr. Damerel now sat, the view extended over a great plain, lighted up with links of the river, and fading into unspeakable hazes of distance, such as were the despair of every artist, and the delight of the fortunate people who lived there and were entertained day by day with the sight of all the sunsets, the midday splendors, the flying shadows, and soft, prolonged twilights. Mr. Damerel was fond of saying that no place he knew so lent itself to idleness as this. "Idleness! I speak as the foolish ones speak," he would say, "for what occupation could be more ennobling than to watch those gleams and shadows—all nature spread out before you, and demanding attention, though so softly that only they who have ears hear? I allow, my gentle nature here does not shout at you, and compel your regard, like her who dwells among the Alps, for instance. My dear, you are always practical—but so long as you leave me my landscape I want little more."

Thus the rector would discourse. It was very little he wanted—only to have his garden and lawn in perfect order, swept and trimmed every morning like a lady's boudoir, and refreshed with every variety of flower: to have his table not heavily loaded with vulgar English joints, but daintily covered, and oh! so daintily served; the linen always fresh, the crystal always fine, the ladies dressed as ladies should be: to have his wine, of which he said he took very little, always fine, of choice vintage, and with a bouquet which rejoiced the heart: to have plenty of new books: to have quiet, undisturbed by the noise of the children, or any other troublesome noise such as broke the harmony of nature: and especially undisturbed by bills and cares, such as, he declared, at once shorten the life and take all pleasure out of it. This was all he required; and surely never man had tastes more moderate, more innocent, more virtuous and refined.

The little scene to which I have thus abruptly introduced the reader took place in the most delicious part of the garden. The deep stillness of noon, was over the sunshiny world; part of the lawn was brilliant in light; the very insects were subdued out of their buzz of activity by the spell of the sunshine; but here, under the lime-tree, there was grateful shade, where everything took breath. Mr. Damerel was seated in a chair which had been made expressly for him, and which combined the comfort of soft cushions with such a rustic appearance as became its habitation out of doors; under his feet was a soft Persian rug in colors blended with all the harmony which belongs to the Eastern loom; at his side a pretty carved table, with a raised rim, with books upon it, and a thin Venice glass containing a rose. Another Rose, the Rose of my story, was half-sitting, half-reclining on the grass at his feet—a pretty, light figure in a soft muslin dress, almost white, with bits of soft, rose-colored ribbon here and there. She was the eldest child of the house. Her features I do not think were at all remarkable, but she had a bloom so soft, so delicate, so sweet, that her father's fond title for her, "a Rose in June," was everywhere acknowledged as appropriate. A rose of the very season of roses was this Rose. Her very smile, which came and went like breath, never away for two minutes together, yet never lasting beyond the time you took to look at her, was flowery too, I can scarcely tell why. For my own part, she always reminded me not so much of a garden-rose in its glory, as of a branch of wild roses all blooming and smiling from the bough, here pink, here white, here with a dozen ineffable tints. Her hair was light-brown with the least little curl in the world just about her forehead, but shining like satin on her pretty head; her eyes too were brown, with a dancing gleam of light in each; the delicate eyebrows curved, the eyelashes curved, the lips curved, all wavy and rounded. Life and light shone out of the girl, and sweet, unconscious happiness. In all her life she had never had any occasion to ask herself was she happy. Of course she was happy! did not she live, and was not that enough? Rose Damerel was the last dainty ornament of his house in which her father delighted most. He had spoiled her lessons when she was younger because of his pleasure in her and her pretty looks, and he interfered now almost altogether with that usefulness in a house which is demanded by every principle of duty from the eldest daughter of a large family; for alas! there was a large family, a thing which was the cause of all trouble to the Damerels. Had there been only Rose, and perhaps one brother, how much more pleasantly would everything have gone! In that case there might have been fewer lines in the brow of the third person whom Mr. Damerel spoke to, but whom the reader has not yet seen.

What Mrs. Damerel was like in her June of life, when she married her husband and was a Rose too, like her daughter, it is difficult to tell. Life, which often makes so little real change, brings out much that is latent both of good and evil. I have said she was a Rose, like her daughter—and so, indeed, she was still, so far as formal documents went; but, somehow or other, the name had gone from her. She had acquired from her husband, at first in joke and loving banter of her early cares of housekeeping, while they were still no more than married lovers, the name of Martha, and by degrees that name had so fastened to her that no one recognized her by any other. Nobody out of her own family knew that it was not her name, and of course the children, some of whom were indignant at the change, could not set it right. In her letters she signed herself "R. M. Damerel"—never Rose; and her correspondents took it for granted that the "M" stood for Martha. That she was careful and troubled about many things was the rector's favorite joke. "My careful wife—my anxious wife," he called her, and, poor soul, not without a cause. For it stands to reason that when a man must not be disturbed about bills, for example, his wife must be, and doubly; when a man cannot bear the noise of children, his wife must, and doubly; and even when a clergyman dislikes poverty, and unlovely cottages, and poor rooms, which are less sweet than the lawn and the roses, why, his wife must, and make up for his fastidiousness. She had eight children, and a husband of the most refined tastes of any clergyman in England, and an income—not so much as might have been desired. Alas! how few of us have so much as might be desired! Good rich people, you who have more money than you want, how good you ought to be to us, out of pure gratitude to Heaven for the fact that you can pay your bills when you like, and never need to draw lines on your forehead with thinking which is imperative and which will wait! Mrs. Damerel was well dressed—she could not help it—for that was one of the rector's simple luxuries. Fortunately, in summer it is not so difficult to be well dressed at a small cost. She had on (if any one cares to know) a dress of that light brown linen which everybody has taken to wearing of late, over an old black silk petticoat, which, having been good once, looked good even when tottering on the brink of the grave. She was no more than forty, and but for her cares, would have looked younger; but June was long over for this Rose, and the lines in her forehead contradicted the softness of the natural curves in her features. Those lines were well ruled in, with rigid straightening, by an artist who is very indifferent to curves and prettiness, and had given a certain closeness, and almost sternness, to the firm-shutting of her mouth. I am afraid, though she had great command of herself, that Mr. Damerel's delightful and unbroken serenity had an irritating effect on his wife, in addition to the effects produced by her burden of care; and irritation works with a finer and more delicate pencil than even anxiety. She had come out this morning to ask Rose's help with the children, to whom, among her other fatigues, she had lately begun to give lessons, finding the daily governess from the village impracticable. She had been called away to other duties, and the children were alone in the school-room. She had just asked her daughter to go in and take charge of them, and I scarcely think—let alone the answer she had just received from her husband—that the sight of this cool, fresh, delightful leisure in direct contrast with the hot house, and the school-room, where all the children were more tiresome than usual by reason of the heat, had any agreeable effect upon Mrs. Damerel's nerves. Such a contrast to one's own frets and annoyances seldom is deeply consolatory.

"Martha, Martha, thou art careful and troubled about many things. Let the child alone!"

The rector smiled, yet his tone was one of playful reproof. His was the superior position. With the soft air fanning him, and the shade refreshing him, and the beautiful landscape displaying itself for him, and all the flowers blooming, the leaves waving, the butterflies fluttering, the pretty daughter prattling, all for his pleasure, master of the creation as he was, he was in a position to reprove any harsh and hasty intruder who brought into this Paradise a discordant note.

"I do not want to burden her youth," said Mrs. Damerel, with a resolute quiet in her voice, which her children knew the sound of, and which they all learned to recognize as the tone of suppressed irritation, "but I think it would do Rose no harm, Herbert, to make herself useful a little, and help me."

"Useful!" he said, with a half-pitying smile; "the other roses are still less useful. What would you have the child do? Let her get the good of this beautiful morning. Besides, she is useful to me."

"Ah," said Mrs. Damerel, faltering slightly, "if she is doing anything for you, Herbert!"

"My dear," said the rector, with a gentle elevation of his eyebrows, "don't confound things which are different. Doing something is your sole idea of human use, I know. No, Rose is doing nothing—it helps me to have her there. She is part of the landscape; suppose you sit down yourself, instead of fretting, and enjoy it."

"Enjoy it!" Mrs. Damerel echoed, with faint irony. She heard already the noise of the school-room growing louder and louder, and Mary, the housemaid, stood at the door, looking out anxiously, shading her eyes from the sun, for the mistress. Some one was waiting, she knew, in the hall, to see her; pray Heaven, not some one with a bill! "I am afraid I must go back to my work," she said, "and I hope you will come to me, Rose, as soon as your papa can spare you. I have no more time now."

Rose stirred uneasily, half-rising, and, with a prick of conscience, made a feeble attempt to detain her. "But, mamma"—she began, as her mother moved away, crossing the broad sunshine of the lawn with hasty steps. Mrs. Damerel did not or would not hear, but went swiftly into the house as they watched her, meeting Mary, who was coming with a message. Her light dress shone out for a moment in the fierce blaze of the sunshine, and then disappeared. When she was out of sight the rector said softly, changing his position with the leisureliness of extreme comfort, putting under-most the leg which had been upper-most, "What a pity that your mother does not see the beauty of repose more than she does! If I had not learnt long ago to take no notice, I don't know what I might not have been worried into by now."

"Mamma never worries any one," said Rose, flushing at once with instantaneous opposition. The more she felt guilty towards her mother, the less she would hear a word to her discredit. She blazed up quite hot and fiery, with a loyalty which was a very good quality in its way, though not so good as helping in the school-room. The father put forth his fine ivory hand, and patted her pretty head.

"Quite right, dear, quite right," he said; "always stand up for your mother. And it is true, she never worries anybody; but I wish she had more perception of the excellence of repose."

"Perhaps if she had, we should not be able to enjoy it so much," said the girl, still giving expression to a slight compunction.

"Very well said, Rose; and it is quite possible you are right again. We should not be so comfortable, and the house would not go on wheels as it does, if she thought more of her own ease. One star differeth from another star in glory," said Mr. Damerel, who was fond of quoting Scripture, almost the only point in him which savored slightly of the church. "At the same time, my Rose in June, when you marry, yourself—as I suppose you will one day—remember that there is nothing that worries a man like being constantly reminded of the struggle and wear and tear that life demands. He has enough of that outside in the world," said the rector, gazing out over the fair prospect before him, and again changing the position of his legs, "without having it thrust upon him in what ought to be the sanctity of his home."

Rose looked at her father with a little dawning wonder mingled with the admiration she felt for him. As a picture, Mr. Damerel was perfect. He had a fine head, with beautiful and refined features, and that paleness which has always been found to be so much more interesting than brighter coloring. He lay half-reclined in his easy-chair, with his eyes dreamily regarding the landscape, and the book he had been reading closed over his hand. That hand was in itself a patent of gentility, and his whole appearance confirmed the title. Somewhat fragile—a piece of delicate porcelain among the rough delf of this world—not able to endure much knocking about; fastidious, loving everything that was beautiful, and supporting with difficulty that which was not, the rector looked like a choice example of the very height of civilization and refinement. And everything around him was in harmony: the velvet lawn on which no fallen leaf was allowed to lie for an hour; the pretty house behind, perfection of English comfort and daintiness; the loose morning clothes, not more than half clerical, and perfectly unpretending, yet somehow more fine, better cut, and better fitting than other people's clothes. Rose had for him that enthusiasm of admiration which a girl often entertains for a handsome and gentle-minded father, who takes the trouble to enter into her feelings, and make her his companion. I do not know any more exquisite sentiment in humanity. She loved him entirely, and he was to her a very model of everything that was most delightful, kind, tender, and beautiful.

But as she looked at this model of man, his words somehow struck and vibrated upon a new chord in the girl's mind. "The struggle and wear and tear that life demands." Did Mr. Damerel have much of that "outside," as he said? He resumed his reading, but his daughter did not look again at the book of poetry which lay open on her knee. Somehow a reflection of the pucker on her mother's brow had got into her heart—her mother, whom Rose loved, but who was not an idol and model of excellence, like the gentle and graceful being at her side. The contrast struck her for perhaps the first time in her life. What was the meaning of it? Was it because Mrs. Damerel did not understand the beauty of repose, or because a woman's business in this world is more detailed and engrossing than a man's? "Fancy mamma spending the whole morning out of doors reading poetry!" Rose said to herself, with an involuntary silent laugh over the absurdity of the notion. No doubt it was because of the difference between man and woman; one of those disabilities which people talked about; and perhaps (Rose went on philosophizing) women are wrong to absorb themselves in this way in the management of their houses, and ought to rule their domestic affairs with a lighter hand, not interfering with all the little minutiæ, and making slaves of themselves. She looked towards the house as she mused, and the vague compunction which had been in her mind sharpened into something like a prick of conscience. It was delightful being out here in the soft shade of the lime-trees, watching when she liked the flitting shadows over the plain below, and the gleam of the river here and there among the trees—reading when she liked "Balaustion's Adventure," which was the book on her knee. The significance of the old story embedded in that book did not for the moment strike her. I think she was, on the whole, rather annoyed with Mr. Browning for having brought down the story of a woman's sacrifice, all for love, into the region of even poetic reason. To Rose, at that period of her development, it seemed the most ideal climax of life to die for the man she loved. What could be more beautiful, more satisfactory? Such an ending would reconcile one, she thought, to any suffering; it gave her heart a thrill of high sensation indescribable in words. How sweet the air was, how lovely all the lights! Rose was just enough of an artist to be able to talk about "the lights" with some faint understanding of what she meant. She was in a kind of soft Elysium, penetrated by the thousand sensations of the morning, the quiet, the flattering soft air that caressed her, the poetry, the society, the beauty all around. But then there came that sharp little prick of conscience. Perhaps she ought to go in and offer the help her mother wanted. Rose did not jump up to do this, as she would have done at once (she felt sure) had she been required to die, like Iphigenia, for her country, or, like Alcestis, for her husband. The smaller sacrifice somehow was less easy; but it disturbed her a little in the perfection of her gentle enjoyment, and dictated a few restless movements which caught her father's eye. He turned and looked at her, asking fretfully, with a look, what was the matter, for he did not like to be disturbed.

"Perhaps," said Rose, inquiringly, and appealing to him with another look, "I ought to go in and see what is wanted. Perhaps I could be of some use to mamma."

Mr. Damerel smiled. "Use?" he said. "Has your mother bitten you with her passion for use? You are not of the useful kind, take my word for it; and make yourself happy, like your namesakes, who toil not, neither do they spin."

"But perhaps"—said Rose softly to herself—her father gave her a friendly little nod and returned to his book—and she had to solve her problem without his assistance. She tried to do it, sitting on the grass, and it was a long and rather troublesome process. It would have been much more easily and briefly settled, had she gone into the school-room; but then I am afraid Rose did not wish it to be solved that way.

CHAPTER II.

Mrs. Damerel went back into the house with a countenance much less placid than that of her husband. I scarcely know why it is that the contrast of perfect repose and enjoyment with anxiety, work, and care should irritate the worker as it invariably does; but here indeed there was reason enough; for Mrs. Damerel felt that the two people luxuriating in total absence of care on this delightful morning ought to have taken a considerable share with her in her labors and lightened the burden she was now obliged to bear alone. This mingled a sharpness of feeling with her toils. People who interpret human nature coarsely—and they are, perhaps, the majority—would have said that Mrs. Damerel was jealous of her husband's preference for Rose's society, and this would have been a total and vulgar mistake; but she had in her mind a feeling which it is difficult to explain, which for the moment made her irritation with Rose more strong than her irritation with Rose's father. He was, in the first place, a man—grand distinction, half contemptuous, half respectful, with which women of Mrs. Damerel's age (I don't say young women often do it, at least consciously—except in the case of their fathers and brothers) account for and make up their minds to so many things. I am not attempting to account for this sentiment, which is so similar to that with which men in their turn regard women; I only acknowledge its existence. He was a man, brought up as all men are (I still quote Mrs. Damerel's thoughts, to which she seldom or never gave expression), to think of themselves first, and expect everything to give in to them. But Rose had none of these privileges. What her mother as a woman had to take upon her, Rose had an equal right to take too. Mrs. Damerel herself could not forget, though everybody else did, that she had been a Rose too, in her proper person; the time even since that miraculous period was not so far off to her as to the others; but before she was Rose's age she had been married, and had already become, to some extent, Mr. Damerel's shield and buckler against the world and its annoyances. And here was Rose growing up as if she, instead of being a woman as nature made her, was herself one of the privileged class, to whom women are the ministers. This annoyed Mrs. Damerel more, perhaps, than the facts justified; it gave her a sense of injured virtue as well as feeling. It would be the ruin of the girl—it was wrong to let her get into such ways. The mother was angry, which is always painful and aggravates everything. She was too proud to struggle with her daughter, or to exact help which was not freely given; for Rose was no longer a child to be sent hither and thither and directed what to do. And Mrs. Damerel was no more perfect than Rose was—she had her own difficulties of temper like other people. This was one of them—that she drew back within herself when she felt her appeal refused or even left without response. She went in with a little scorn, a little pride, a good deal of anger and more of mortification. "I must do everything myself, it appears," she said, with a swelling of the heart which was very natural, I think. After the sun on the lawn, it was very warm in-doors and the school-room was very noisy indeed by the time she had got rid of the applicants in the hall, one of whom (most respectful and indeed obsequious, and perfectly willing to accept her excuses, but yet a dun notwithstanding) had come to say that he had many heavy payments to make up, etc.—and if Mrs. Damerel could oblige him—Mrs. Damerel could not oblige him, but he was very civil and full of apologies for troubling her.

I do not, by any means, intend to say that the rector's wife was tortured by perpetual struggling with her creditors. It was not so bad as that. The difficulty was rather to keep going, to be not too much in debt to any one, to pay soon enough to preserve her credit, and yet get as long a day as possible. Mrs. Damerel had come by long practice to have the finest intuition in such matters. She knew exactly how long a tailor or a wine merchant would wait for his money without acerbation of temper, and would seize that crowning moment to have him paid by hook or by crook. But by thus making a fine art of her bills, she added infinitely to her mental burdens—for a woman must never forget anything or neglect anything when she holds her tradespeople so very delicately in hand.

The school-room, as I have just said, was very noisy, not to say uproarious, when she got back to it, and it was hard not to remember that Rose ought to have been there. There were five children in it, of various ages and sizes. The two big boys were both at Eton. The eldest, Bertie, who was bright and clever, was "on the foundation," and therefore did not cost his parents much; the second had his expenses paid by a relation—thus these two were off their mother's hands. The eldest in the school-room was Agatha, aged fourteen, who taught the two little ones; but who, during her mother's absence, ought to have been playing "her scales," and had conscientiously tried to do so for ten minutes, at the end of which time she had been obliged to resign the music in order to rescue these same two little ones, her special charge, from the hands of Dick, aged ten, who was subjecting them to unknown tortures, which caused the babes to howl unmercifully. Patty, the next girl to Agatha, aided and abetted Dick; and what with the laughter of these two pickles, and the screams of the small ones, and poor Agatha's remonstrances, the scene was Pandemonium itself, and almost as hot; for the room was on the sunny side of the house, and blazing, notwithstanding the drawn blinds.

The children were all languid and irritable with the heat, hating their confinement in-doors; and, indeed, if Rose had come, she would have made a very poor exchange. Agatha's music had tumbled down from the piano, the old red cover was half drawn off the table, and threatened at any moment a clean sweep of copybooks, inkbottles and slates. Dick stood among his books, all tumbled on the floor, his heels crushing the cover of one, while Patty sat upon the open dictionary, doubling down half the leaves with her weight. Such a scene for a bothered mother to come into! Mr. Damerel himself heard some faint rumor of the noise, and his fine brow had begun to draw itself into lines, and a resolution to "speak to their mother" formed itself within his mind. Poor mother! She could have cried when she went in out of all her other troubles; but that was a mere momentary weakness, and the rebels were soon reduced to order, Agatha sent back to her scales, and Dick and Patty to their copybooks. "You two little ones may go," Mrs. Damerel said, and with a shriek of delight the babies toddled out and made their way to the hayfield behind the house, where they were perfectly happy, and liable to no more danger than that of being carried off in a load of fragrant hay. When Mr. Nolan, the curate, came in to talk about parish business, Agatha's "scales," not badly played, were trilling through the place, and Patty and Dick, very deep in ink, and leaning all their weight upon their respective pens, were busy with their writing; and calm—the calm of deep awe—prevailed.

"Shall I disturb you if I come in here?" asked the curate, with a mellow sound in his voice which was not brogue—or at least he thought it was not, and was ingenuously surprised when he was recognized as an Irishman. ("It will be my name, to be sure," he would say on such occasions, somewhat puzzled.) He was a bony man, loosely put together, in a long coat, with rather a wisp of a white tie; for, indeed, it was very hot and dusty on the roads, and where the rector is an elegant man of very refined mind, the curate, like the wife, has generally a good deal to do.

"Indeed, the lessons have been so much disturbed as it is, that it does not much matter," said Mrs. Damerel. "On Monday morning there are so many things to call me away."

"How selfish of me!" said the curate. "Monday morning is just the time I've little or nothing to do, except when there's sickness. What a brute I was not to offer meself,—and indeed, that's just what I've come to speak about."

"No, no, you are too kind, and do too much already," said Mrs. Damerel, looking at him with a grateful smile, but shaking her head. "And, indeed," she added, the cloud coming over her face again, "Rose ought to come and relieve me; but her father has to be attended to, and that takes up so much of her time."

"To be sure," said the curate cheerily, "and reason good. Besides, it would be wearing work for one like her—whereas the like o' me is made for it. Look here, Dick, my boy, will you promise to learn your lessons like a brick to-morrow if I ask the mother for a holiday to-day?"

"Oh, hurrah!" cried Dick, delighted.

"Oh, mamma, like twenty bricks," cried Patty, "though how a brick can learn lessons?—It's so hot, and one keeps thinking of the hayfield."

"Then be off wi' you all," cried the curate. "Don't you see the mother smile? and Agatha too. I'm going to talk business. Sure, you don't mind for one day?"

"Oh, mind!" said poor Mrs. Damerel, with a half-smile; then waiting till they were all out of hearing, an exit speedily accomplished, "if it were not for duty, how glad I should be to give it up altogether!—but they could not go on with Miss Hunt," she added, with a quick glance at the curate to see whether by chance he understood her. Good curate, he could be very stolid on occasion, though I hope he was not fool enough to be taken in by Mrs. Damerel's pretences: though it was true enough that Miss Hunt was impracticable. She could not afford a better; this was what she really meant.

"Out of the question," said Mr. Nolan; "and I'm no scholar myself to speak of, notwithstanding what I'm going to have the presumption to say to you. It's just this—I don't do much visiting of mornings; they don't like it. It takes them all in a mess as it were, before they've had time to get tidy, and these mornings hang heavy on my hands. I want you to let me have the three big ones. I might get them on a bit; and time, as I tell you, my dear lady, hangs heavy on my hands."

"How can you tell me such a fib?" said Mrs. Damerel, half crying, half laughing. "Oh, you are too good, too good; but, Mr. Nolan, I can't take anything more from you. Rose must help me, it is her duty; it is bad for her to be left so much to herself; why, I was married and had all the troubles of life on my head at her age."

"And so she'll have, before you know where you are," said the good curate, which will show the reader at once that he entertained no absorbing passion for Miss Rose, though I am aware it is a curate's duty so to do. "So she'll have; she'll be marrying some great grandee or other. She looks like a princess, and that's what she'll be."

"She has no right to be a princess," said the mother, overwrought and irritable, "and duty is better than ease surely. You, I know, think so."

"For the like of me, yes," said the curate; "for her, I don't know."

"I was once very much like her, though you would not think it," said the mother, with the slightest tinge of bitterness, "but that is not the question—no, no, we must not trouble you."

"When I tell you the mornings hang on my hands! I don't know what to do with my mornings. There's Tuesday I'm due at the schools, but the rest of the week I do nothing but idle. And idling's a great temptation. A cigar comes natural when you've nothing to do. You don't like a man smoking in the morning; I've heard you say so. So you see the young ones will save me from a—no, I won't say cigar; worse than that; cigars are too dear for a curate, me dear lady—from a pipe."

"Mr. Nolan, you are too good for this world," said poor Mrs. Damerel, affected to tears; "but I must first try what can be done at home," she added after a pause; "no, no, you weigh me down under your kindness. What would the parish be but for you?"

"It would be just the same if I were dead and buried," said the curate, shrugging his shoulders. "Ah, that's the worst of it: try for a little bit of a corner of work like a child's lessons, and you may be of service; but try to mend the world, even a bit of a parish, and you're nowhere. They don't think half as much of me as they do of the rector?" he added, with a curious smile, which the rector's wife only half understood. Was it satirical? or could it be possible that the curate was surprised that the people thought more of the rector than of himself? Mrs. Damerel was aware, no one better, of her husband's faults. Many a time she was ready to say in bitterness (to herself) that he was wearing her to death; but nevertheless she looked at long, loosely-built, snub-nosed Mr. Nolan, with mingled amusement and surprise. Was it possible that he could entertain any hopes of rivalling her husband? Of course a visit from the rector was an honor to any one, for Mr. Damerel was a man who, notwithstanding a little human weakness, was the very picture and model of a gentleman; and the idea of comparing him with good Mr. Nolan was too absurd.

"Yes, no doubt they are pleased to see him," she said: "poor people are very quick to recognize high breeding; but I am sure, my dear Mr. Nolan, that they are all very fond of you."

The curate made no immediate answer. I am not sure that he had not in his private heart something of the same feeling with which his present companion had been thinking of her daughter, a feeling less intense in so far as it was much more indifferent to him, yet in a way stronger because untempered by affection. The rector was of his own kind, the ornamental and useless specimen, while he was the worker whom nobody thought of; but these secret feelings neither of the two confided to the other. Mr. Nolan would have been horrified had he detected in Mrs. Damerel that slight bitterness about Rose, which indeed would have shocked herself as deeply had she paused to identity the sentiment, and she would have been, and was, to some slight extent—suspecting the existence of the feeling—contemptuous and indignant of Nolan's "jealousy," as I fear she would have called it. They returned, however, to the educational question, which did not involve anything painful, and after considerable discussion it was settled that he should give the elder children lessons in the morning "if their papa approved." It is impossible to say what a relief this decision was to the mother, who had felt these lessons to be the last straw which proverbially breaks the camel's back. She was glad of the chat with a sympathizing friend, who understood, without saying anything about, her troubles—and doubly glad of the holiday exacted from her by his means—and gladder still to get rid of him and return to her many other occupations; for it was Monday, as has already been mentioned, and there was the laundress to look after, and a thousand other things awaiting her. The curate went out by the garden door when he left her, out upon the lawn, where he paused to look at as charming a scene as could be found in England: a fair country spreading out for miles its trees and fields and soft undulations under a summer sky, which was pale with excess of light, and ran into faint lines of misty distance almost colorless in heat and haze. Here and there the sunshine caught in a bend of the river, and brought out a startling gleam as from a piece of silver. The world was still with noon and distance, no sound in the air but the rustle of the leaves, the hum of insects; the landscape was all the sweeter that there was no remarkable feature in it, nothing but breadth and space, and undulating lines, and light, everywhere light; and to make up for its broad, soft vagueness, how distinct, like a picture, was the little group in the foreground—the lime-trees in their silken green, the soft rippling shadows on the grass, the picturesque figure in the chair, and the beautiful girl!

The beauty of the sight charmed good Mr. Nolan. Had it been put to him at that moment, I believe he would have protested that his rector should never do anything in his life except recline with languid limbs outstretched, and his poetical head bent over his book, under the sweet shadow of the trees. And if this was true even in respect to Mr. Damerel, how much more true was it with Rose?

"Well, Nolan," said Mr. Damerel, suavely, as the bony curate and his shadow came stalking across the sunshine; "well, worrying yourself to death as usual in this hot weather? My wife and you are congenial souls."

"That is true, and it's a great honor for me," said Nolan. "*She* is worrying herself to death with the children, and one thing and another. As for me, in the mornings, as I tell her, I've next to nothing to do."

Rose looked up hastily as he spoke. How angry she felt! If her mother chose to worry herself to death, who had anything to do with that? was it not her own pleasure? A hot flush came over the girl's face. Mr. Nolan thought it was the quick, ingenuous shame which is so beautiful in youth; but it was a totally different sentiment.

"Mamma does nothing she does not choose to do," she cried; then blushed more hotly, perceiving vaguely that there was something of self-defense in the heat with which she spoke.

Mr. Nolan was not graceful in his manners, like Mr. Damerel, but he had that good breeding which comes from the heart, and he changed the subject instantly, and began to talk to the rector of parish business, over which Mr. Damerel yawned with evident weariness. "Excuse me; the heat makes one languid," he said. "You have my full sanction, Nolan. You know how entirely I trust to your discretion; indeed, I feel that you understand the people in some respects better than I do. Don't trouble yourself to enter into details."

Mr. Nolan withdrew from these refined precincts with an odd smile upon his face, which was not half so handsome as Mr. Damerel's. He had the parish in his hands, and the rector did not care to be troubled with details; but the rector had all the advantages of the position, all the income, and even so much the moral superiority over his curate, that even *they* (by which pronoun Mr. Nolan indicated his poorer parishioners) felt much more deeply honored by a chance word from the rector than they did by his constant ministrations and kindness.

What an odd, unequal world this is! he was thinking of himself—not ruled by justice, or even a pretence at justice, but by circumstances alone and external appearances. This did not make him bitter, for he had a kind of placid philosophy in him, and was of the kind of man who takes things very easily, as people say; but the curious force of the contrast made him smile.

CHAPTER III.

Rose Damerel's life had, up to this time, been spent altogether in the sunshine. She had been too young when she went to school to ponder much over anything that went on at home, and had concluded during her holidays that home, which was so dainty, so pleasant, so sweet, was a kind of paradise on earth, infinitely more delightful than any of the other homes of which she heard from her school-fellows. None of them had a father so delightful, a mother so kind; and in these holiday times, as everybody indulged and petted her, the private shadows—I will not say skeletons—in the house were never divined by her. She had, as sometimes happens to the eldest of a large family, much more care taken of her education and training than her sisters were likely to meet with. The burden had not begun to be so heavily felt when the eldest girl grew into bright intelligence, to her parents' pride. The others were still too young to demand or even to suggest the expense that would be involved in their education—and nothing was spared upon Rose. She had returned from school not much more than a year before the time of which I treat, and had gone on for some time in her delightful youthful confidence that everything around her was exactly as it ought to be. But shadows had begun to flit vaguely across the picture before that memorable day in the garden, which henceforward became a turning point in her thoughts. This was the first moment at which she fully identified the occasional clouds upon her mother's face, and learned that Mrs. Damerel was not merely a little cross—that easy and rapid solution with which a child settles all problems concerning its parents—but had a distinct cause for the little irritabilities which she tried so carefully to restrain. Perhaps it was in the very nature of things that Rose should be more attracted by the gentle indulgence and indolent perfection of her father than by her mother's stronger character. Mr. Damerel, had he been very rich, and free of all occasion to think of his children's future, would have been a model father to grown-up and well-behaved sons and daughters. He could not bear any roughness, coarseness, or disorderliness, therefore the school-boys were but little congenial to him, and he was never sorry when the holidays were over. And the little children were too troublesome and too noisy to please him; but Rose was the perfection of a child to such a man, and to her he was the perfection of a father. Everything in her pleased and gratified him. She was pretty, gentle, full of intelligence, eager to read with him if he would, still more eager to hear him talk, yet quick to perceive when he was disinclined to talk, and regarding all his moods with religious respect.

She would sit by him for hours together, like a charming piece of still-life, when he pleased, and was ready to converse or to listen, to walk, to sing, to follow his lead in everything, as only a woman-child, full of the beautiful enthusiasm of youthful admiration, can do. Nothing except perhaps the devotion of a young wife, when she really loves the man much older than herself, whom she has married, can equal the devotion of a girl to her father. She admired everything about him—his beautiful refined head, his fine voice, his grace and high breeding, his sermons, and what she called his genius. To find this faultless father to be anything less than a demi-god was terrible to Rose. I do not mean to say that she got within a hundred miles of this discovery all at once; nay, the first result of the vague and dreamy doubts that stole into her mind was rather an increase of enthusiasm for her father, an instinctive making-up to her own ideal for the sense of failure in him, of which she was vaguely conscious. Rose loved her mother after a totally different fashion, in an ordinary and matter-of-fact way, but she had no romance of feeling towards her; and when her whole little world, began, as it were, to sway upon its axis, to yield beneath her feet, as if it might swing round altogether in space, turning what she had supposed the brighter side into shadow, and elevating that which she had held lowly enough, she, poor girl, grew giddy with this strange and sickening sensation. She was at the age, too, when everything is apt to reel about the young experimentalist taking her first steps in life. She was vaguely conscious of being now a free agent, consulted as to her own movements, no longer told curtly to do this and that, but exercising personal choice as to what she should do. This change is of itself sufficiently bewildering. Nature makes, as it were, a pause at this first crisis of personal life. The child, wondering, half-delighted and half-troubled to have no longer its duties clearly and sharply indicated, falls into a partial trance, and neglects many things for sheer want of use and knowledge how to act for itself.

This was Rose's position. Between the mother, who, a little mortified and hurt at her child's want of sympathy with her, did not give her orders, but only suggested employment, and the father, who said, "Never mind, let her alone," she stood, not knowing how to settle the question, but inclining naturally to the side on which she was most indulged and smiled upon, though with a secret uneasiness which she could not shake off, and moral sense of a false situation which grew upon her day by day.

Rose had lovers, too, in this new, miraculous life upon which she had entered: two lovers, not yet declared, but very evident to all knowing eyes; and in the village there were many keen observers. One of these suitors was the most wealthy proprietor, in the neighborhood—a man much above her own age, yet not old, and perfectly qualified to please a lady's eye; and the other, a young naval lieutenant without a penny, the son of Mrs. Wodehouse, who lived on the Green, and had nothing in the world but her pension as an officer's widow. Of course I do not need to say that it was the poor man whom Rose preferred. She was not in love with him—far from it; but she was so completely on the verge of universal awakening, that a word or touch might be enough to arouse her whole being at any moment—might open her eyes to her own position and that of her parents, and show her the nature of her individual sentiments, as by a sudden gleam of light. Rose, however, was not the least in the world aware of this; and at the present moment she was no further advanced than was consistent with saying frankly that she liked Wodehouse very much—and feeling (but of this she said nothing) more glad when she saw him coming than about any other event in her simple days.

Dinglefield is a sociable place, and there is something in a soft summer evening after a very hot, blazing summer day which fosters a disposition to stroll about and interchange greetings with your neighbors. As it began to darken upon the evening of this particular day, various people in the houses about stepped out of their wide-open windows after dinner, and, tempted by the beauty of twilight, strayed along the road or over the Green to the rectory garden, which was by universal acknowledgment "the most perfect spot" in the village. Much has been said about the charms of twilight, but little, I think, of its peculiar English beauty, which is not so magical as the momentary interval between light and dark in the south, or the lingering, prolonged, silvery, and ineffable dimness of those northern twilights which last half the night; but has a dusky softness altogether peculiar to itself, like the shadowing of downy wings. The air was delicious, fresh after the hot day, yet so warm as to make wrappings quite unnecessary. The sky, still somewhat pale in its blue after the languor of the heat, looked down faint yet friendly, as if glad to see again a little movement and sense of life. A few subdued stars peeped out here and there, and the wide stretch of country lay dim underneath, revealing itself in long soft lines of gray, till it struck into a higher tone of blue on the horizon where earth and heaven met. All the Damerels who were out of bed were in the garden, and the neighbors, who had made this pleasant terrace the end of their walk, were scattered about in various groups. Mr. Incledon, who was Rose's wealthy lover, came late and stood talking with Mrs. Damerel, watching with wistful eyes her appropriation by his rival, young Wodehouse—whose mother, hooded in the white Shetland shawl, which she had thrown over her cap to come out, sat on a garden-chair with her feet upon the rector's Persian rug, listening to him while he talked, with the devout admiration which became a member of his flock. The rector was talking politics with General Peronnet, and Mrs. Wodehouse thought it was beautiful to see how thoroughly he understood a subject which was so much out of his way as the abolition of purchase in the army. "If he had been in parliament now!" she said to the general's wife, who thought her husband was the object of the eulogy. There were two or three other members of this group listening to the rector's brilliant talk, saying a few words, wise or foolish, as occasion served. Others were walking about upon the lawn, and one lady, with her dress lifted, was hastening off the grass which she had just discovered to be wet with dew. Upon none of them, however, did Mr. Incledon's attention turn. He followed with his eyes a pair whose young figures grew less and less in the distance, half lost in the darkness. The persistence with which he watched them seemed a reproach to the mother, with whom he talked by fits and starts, and whose anxiety was not at all awakened by the fact that Rose was almost out of sight. "I am afraid Rose is not so careful as she ought to be about the dew on the grass," she said, half apologetically, half smiling, in reply to his look.

"Shall I go and tell her you think so?" said Mr. Incledon, hastily. He was a man of about five-and-thirty, good looking, sensible, and well dispositioned; a personage thoroughly *comme il faut*. He was the sort of suitor whom proper parents love to see approaching a favorite child. He could give his wife everything a woman could desire—provide for her handsomely, surround her with luxury, fill her life with pleasures and prettinesses, and give her an excellent position. And the man himself was free of cranks and crotchets, full of good sense, well educated, good tempered. Where are girls' eyes, that they do not perceive such advantages? Mrs. Damerel hesitated a moment between sympathy with her child and sympathy with this admirable man. There was a struggle in her mind which was to have the predominance. At length some gleam of recollection or association struck her, and moved the balance in Rose's favor, who she felt sure did not want Mr. Incledon just at that moment.

"Never mind," she said tranquilly, "it will not hurt her;" and resumed a conversation about the music in the church, which was poor. Mr. Incledon was very musical, but he had no more heart for anthems at that moment than had he never sung a note.

Rose had strayed a little way down the slope with Edward Wodehouse. They were not talking much, and what they did say was about nothing in particular—the garden, the wild flowers among the grass on this less polished and less cultured lawn which sloped down the little hill. At the moment when the elder suitor's glances had directed Mrs. Damerel's attention towards them they were standing under a gnarled old hawthorn-tree, round which was a little platform of soft turf.

"We lose the view lower down," said Rose; and there they stopped accordingly, neither of them caring to turn back. The soft plain stretched away in long lines before them into the haze and distance like the sea. And as they stood there, the young moon, which had been hidden behind a clump of high trees, suddenly glinted out upon them with that soft, dewy glimmer which makes the growing crescent so doubly sweet. They were both a little taken aback, as if they had been surprised by some one suddenly meeting and looking at them—though indeed there was not a syllable of their simple talk that all the world might not have heard. Both made a step on as if to return again after this surprise, and then they both laughed, with a little innocent embarrassment, and turned back to the view.

"What a lovely night!" said Rose, with a faint little sigh. She had already said these not remarkable words two or three times at least, and she had nothing in the world to sigh about, but was in fact happier than usual; though a little sad, she knew not why.

"Look at those lights down below there," said young Wodehouse; "how they shine out among the trees!"

"Yes, that is from Ankermead,", said Rose; "you know it?—the prettiest little house!"

"When we are away, we poor mariners," he said, with a little laugh which was more affected than real, "that is, I think, the thing that goes to our hearts most."

"What?"

"The lights in the windows—of course I don't mean at sea," said young Wodehouse; "but when we are cruising about a strange coast, for instance, just one of those twinkles shining out of the darkness—you can see lights a long way off—gives a fellow a stab, and makes him think of home."

"But it is pleasant to think of home," said Rose. "Oh, what am I saying? I beg your pardon, Mr. Wodehouse. To be sure, I know what you mean. When I was at school something used to come in my throat when I remembered—many a time I have stood at the window, and pretended I was looking out, and cried."

"Ah!" said Wodehouse, half sympathetic, half smiling, "but then you know it would not do if I looked over the ship's side and cried—though I have had a great mind to do it sometimes, in my midshipman days."

"To cry is a comfort," said Rose; "what do you men do, instead?"

"We smoke, Miss Damerel; and think. How often I shall think of this night and the lights yonder, and mix up this sweet evening with an interior, perhaps sweeter still!"

"I don't think so," said Rose, with a soft laugh, in which there was, however, a shade of embarrassment which somewhat surprised herself. "The room is rather stuffy, and the lamps not bright, if you were near enough; and two old people half dozing over the tea-table, one with the newspaper, one with her worsted-work. It is very humdrum, and not sweet at all inside."

"Well, perhaps they are all the fonder of each other for being humdrum; and it must have been sweet when they were young."

"They were never young," said Rose, with a silvery peal of laughter, turning to go back to the lawn. "See what tricks imagination plays! You would not like to spend an evening there, though the lights are so pretty outside."

"Imagination will play many a trick with me before I forget it," said young Wodehouse in subdued tones. Rose's heart fluttered a little—a very little—with the softest preliminary sensations of mingled happiness and alarm. She did not understand the flutter, but somehow felt it right to fly from it, tripping back to the serenity of society on the lawn. As for the young man, he had a great longing to say something more, but a feeling which was mingled of reverence for her youth and dread of frightening her by a premature declaration kept him silent.

He followed her into the hum of friendly talk, and then across the lawn to the house, where the neighbors streamed in for tea. The bright lights in the rectory drawing-room dazzled them both—the windows were wide open; crowds of moths were flickering in and out, dashing themselves, poor suicides, against the circle of light; and all the charmed dimness grew more magical as the sky deepened into night, and the moon rose higher and began to throw long shadows across the lawn. "On such a night" lovers once prattled in Shakespeare's sweetest vein. All that they said, and a great deal more, came into young Wodehouse's charmed heart and stole it away. He heard himself saying the words, and wondered how it was that he himself was so entirely happy and sad, and thought how he might perhaps soon say them to himself as his ship rustled through the water, and the moonlight slept broad and level and uninterrupted by any poetry of shadows upon the sea. To think of that filled his heart with a soft, unspeakable pang; and yet the very pain had a sweetness in it, and sense of exaltation. "There are the lights still," he said, standing over her where she had seated herself near the window. "I shall always remember them, though you will not allow of any romance"—

"Romance! oh no," said Rose lightly; "only two old people. We have not any romance here."

Mr. Incledon, who had been watching his opportunity so long, now came forward with a cup of tea. Poor Edward was too much abstracted in his thoughts and in her, and with the confusion of a little crisis of sentiment, to think of the usual attentions of society which he owed to her. He started and blushed when he saw how negligent he had been, and almost stumbled over her chair in his anxiety to retrieve his carelessness. "My dear Wodehouse, Miss Damerel cannot drink more than one cup of tea at a time," said the elder suitor, with that air of indulgent pity for his vagaries which so irritates a young man; and he mounted guard over Rose for the rest of the evening. The good neighbors began to go home when they had taken their tea, and the rector and his daughter went with them to the gate, when there was a soft babble and commotion of good nights, and every two people repeated to each other, "What a lovely moon!" and "What a glorious night!" As for poor Wodehouse, in his climax of youth and love, his very heart was melted within him. Twice he turned back, murmuring to his mother some inarticulate explanation that he had forgotten something—that he wanted to speak to the rector—and twice went back to her solemnly saying it did not matter. "No, no," he said to himself, "he must not be premature."

Rose took another turn round the lawn with her father before they went in. Mrs. Damerel was visible inside, sending the tray away, putting stray books in their places, and stray bits of work in the work-basket, before the bell should ring for prayers. Mr. Damerel looked in as he passed with an indulgent smile.

"She calleth her maidens about her," he said, "though it is not to spin, Rose, but to pray. Somehow it enhances the luxury of our stroll to see your mother there, putting everything in order with that careful and troubled face—eh, child, don't you think with me?"

"But does it enhance her luxury to have us walking and talking while she has everything to lay by?" said Rose with an uncomfortable sense that her own work and several books which she had left about were among those which her mother was putting away.

"Ah, you have found out that there are two sides to a question," said her father, patting her on the cheek, with his gentle habitual smile; but he gave no answer to her question; and then the maids became visible, trooping in, in their white caps and aprons, and the rector with a sigh and a last look at the midnight and the dim, dewy landscape, went in to domesticity and duty, which he did not like so well.

Rose went to her room that night with a thrill of all her gentle being which she could not explain. She looked out from her window among the honeysuckles, and was so disappointed as almost to cry when she found the lights out, and the little cottage on Ankermead lost in the darkness. She could have cried, and yet but for that fanciful trouble, how happy the child was! Everything embraced her—the clinging tendrils of the honeysuckle, so laden with dew and sweetness; the shadows of the trees, which held out their arms to her; the soft, caressing moon which touched her face and surrounded it with a pale glory. Nothing but good and happiness was around, behind, before her, and a trembling of happiness to come, even sweeter than anything she had ever known, whispered over her in soft, indefinite murmurs, like the summer air in the petals of a flower. She opened her bosom to it, with a delicious half-consciousness fresh as any rose that lets its leaves be touched by the sweet south. This Rose in June expanded, grew richer, and of a more damask rosiness, but could not tell why.

CHAPTER IV.

Mrs. Damerel thought it her duty, a few nights after this, to speak to her husband of Rose's suitors. "Mr. Incledon has spoken so plainly to me that I cannot mistake him," she said; "and in case you should not have noticed it yourself, Herbert"—

"I notice it!" he said, with a smile; "what chance is there that I should notice it? So my Rose in June is woman enough to have lovers of her own!"

"I was married before I was Rose's age," said Mrs. Damerel.

"So you were, Martha. I had forgotten the progress of time, and that summer, once attained, is a long step towards autumn. Well, if it must be, it must be. Incledon is not a bad fellow, as men go."

"But, I think—there is another, Herbert."

"Another!" said the rector, leaning back in his chair with gentle laughter. "Why, this is too good; and who may he be—the No. 2?"

"It is young Wodehouse, the sailor"—

"The widow's son on the Green! Come now, Martha, once for all this is absurd," said Mr. Damerel, suddenly rousing himself up. "This is out of the question: I say nothing against Incledon; but if you have been so foolishly romantic as to encourage a beggar like young Wodehouse"—

"I have not encouraged him. I disapprove of it as much as you can do," said Mrs. Damerel, with a flush on her cheek; "but whether Rose will agree with us I dare not say."

"Oh, Rose!" said her husband, dropping into his easy tone; "Rose is a child; she will follow whatever lead is given to her. I am not afraid of Rose. You must speak to her, and show her which way you intend her mind to go; be very plain and unequivocal; an unawakened mind always should be treated in the plainest and most distinct way."

"But, Herbert—you have more influence than I have ever had over her. Rose is more your companion than mine. I am not sure that it is the best thing for her, so far as practical life is concerned"—

"My dear," said Mr. Damerel, benignly, "Rose has nothing to do with practical life. You women are always excessive, even in your virtues. I do not mean to throw any doubt upon your qualities as the most excellent of wives; but you have not the discrimination to perceive that duties that suit you admirably would be quite out of place in her. It is a matter of natural fitness. The practical is adapted to forty, but not to nineteen. Let the child alone, my love, to enjoy her youth."

"I think you argue like a Jesuit, Herbert," said Mrs. Damerel; "but whether you are right or wrong on this point does not affect what I ask—which is, that you would speak to her. She is much more likely to attend to you than to me."

"Who—I?" said Mr. Damerel, with a fretful line in his fine forehead. "It is totally out of the question, Martha. *I* speak to Rose about her lovers! It would be quite indelicate, in the first place; and in the second, it would be most disagreeable to me."

"But still we have a duty to our child, even if it is disagreeable," said his wife, not willing to give up her object without a struggle.

"My dear Martha, spare me! I knew you would say something about duty. You are very didactic, my love, by nature; but this, you must remember, is rather a reversal of positions between you and me. Let Rose see," he continued, once more relaxing in tone, "that her path is quite clear before her. Incledon is a very good fellow; he will be of use to me in many ways. Nothing could be more desirable. There is a new box of books which I must look over, Martha; do not let me detain you. You will manage the matter admirably, I am sure, in your own sensible way."

And the rector lighted his wife's candle, and opened the door for her with a suavity and almost gallantry which would have brought tears to the eyes of the parish, had they been there to see. "How perfect Mr.

Damerel's behavior is to that rather common-place wife!" Such was the kind of thing people said. He went to look over his box of books from the London library after his talk, with much amusement in his mind as to Rose's lovers. He thought his child perfect as a child; but the idea that a serious man like Incledon should think of her in the serious position of a wife, tickled the rector's fancy. He thought over the matter as he glanced at the books which had been unpacked for him, leaving nothing for his delicate ivory hands to do but turn the volumes over. There was an agreeable and a disagreeable side to it. Incledon, for one thing, would be a capable referee in all money matters, and would help to arrange about the boys and get them on in the world, which was a great relief to think of; for ere now Mr. Damerel had felt the painful reflection thrust upon him, that some time or other he must do something about the boys. The other side of the question was, that he would lose the society of his Rose in June, his pretty companion, whose ornamental presence lent a new charm to his pretty house. He shrugged his shoulders a little over this, saying to himself that it must be sooner or later, and that, after all, he had done without Rose for many years, and had been much of a sufferer in consequence. It was the way of the world; and then he smiled again at the thought of Rose in the serious position of Mr. Incledon's wife.

Mrs. Damerel had very different feelings on the subject as she went upstairs with the candle he had so politely lighted for her, in her hand. I am afraid she was not so softened as she ought to have been by his charming politeness, which made her slightly angry, and she was deeply disturbed by the task he had thrown back upon her. Mrs. Damerel knew that girls were not so easily moulded as their fathers sometimes think. She felt by instinct that, according to all precedent, Wodehouse, who was young and gay and penniless, must be the favorite. She knew, too, that to endeavor to turn the current in favor of the other was almost enough to decide matters against him; and, beyond all this, Mrs. Damerel felt it hard that everything that was painful and disagreeable should be left on her shoulders. Rose was separated from her; she was her father's companion; she was being trained to prefer refined but useless leisure with him to the aid and sympathy which her mother had a right to look for; yet, when it came to be needful to do any disagreeable duty for Rose, it was the mother who had to put herself in the breach. It was hard upon Mrs.

Damerel. All the reproof, the unpleasant suggestions of duty, the disagreeable advice, the apparent exactions to come from her side; while nothing but indulgence, petting, and fondness, and unlimited compliance with every desire she had, should be apparent on the side of the father. I think Mrs. Damerel was right, and that hers was a very hard case indeed.

The Wodehouses came hastily to the rectory the very next day to intimate the sad news of Edward's approaching departure. His mother fairly broke down, and cried bitterly. "I hoped to have had him with me so much longer," she said; "and now he must go off about this slave-trade. Oh! why should we take it upon us to look after everybody, when they don't want to be looked after? If those poor African wretches cared as much for it as we suppose, wouldn't they take better care of themselves? What have we to do, always interfering? When I think of my boy, who is all I have in the world, going out to that dreadful coast, to risk his life for the sake of some one he never saw or heard of"—

"My dear lady, we cannot be altogether guided by private motives," said the rector; "we must take principle for something. Were we to permit the slave-trade, we should depart from all our traditions. England has always been the guardian of freedom."

"Oh, Mr. Damerel!" said the poor lady, with tears in her eyes, "freedom is all very well to talk about, and I suppose it's a great thing, to have; but what is freedom to these poor savages, that it should cost me and other women our boys?"

"It will not cost you your boy," said Mrs. Damerel; "he will come back. Don't take the gloomiest view of the question. He has been there before, and it did not hurt him; why should it now?"

"Ah! who can tell that?" said poor Mrs. Wodehouse, drying her eyes. She was a woman who liked the darker side of all human affairs, and she felt it almost an insult to her when any one prognosticated happiness. Her son was doing all he could to bear up under the depressing influence of her predictions and his regret at leaving her, and disappointment in having his holiday shortened—along with a deeper reason still which he said nothing about. He tried to be as cheerful as he could; but when he turned to Rose and met the one piteous look the girl gave him, and saw her lip quiver—though he did not know whether it was out of sympathy with his mother, or from any personal feeling of her own—he very nearly broke down. He had still ten days to make his preparations for leaving, and before that time he thought to himself he must surely find out whether Rose cared anything for him more than she did for the others whom she had known like him almost all her life. He looked anxiously into her face when he shook hands with her; but Rose, feeling, she could not tell why, more inclined to cry than she had ever been before, without any reason, as she said, would not meet his looks. "This is not my farewell visit," he said, with an attempt at a laugh. "I don't know why I should feel so dismal about it; I shall see you all again."

"Oh, many times, I hope!" said Mrs. Damerel, who could not help feeling kindly towards the poor young fellow, notwithstanding her conspiracy against his interests. The rector did not commit himself in this foolish way, but took leave of the young sailor solemnly. "However that may be," he said, "God bless you, Edward; I am sure you will do your duty, and be a credit to all that wish you well."

This address chilled poor Wodehouse more and more. Was it his dismissal? He tried to bear up against that too, talking of the garden party he was coming to on Wednesday, and of the repeated visits he still hoped for; but, somehow, from the moment he received the rector's blessing he believed in these farewell visits and the explanations they might give rise to, no more. When he went away with his mother, Rose ran up-stairs on some pretext, and her father and mother were left alone.

"Martha," said the rector, "your usual careful solicitude failed you just now. You as good as asked him to come back; and what could possibly be so bad for Rose?"

"How could I help it?" she said. "Poor boy, he must come again, at least to say good-by."

"I don't see the necessity. It will only make mischief. Rose is quite cast down, whether from sympathy or from feeling. We should take care not to be at home when he calls again."

Mr. Damerel said this in so even a voice that it was delightful to hear him speak, and he went out and took his seat under the lime-trees as a man should who has discharged all his duties and is at peace and in favor with both God and man. Rose did not venture to face her mother with eyes which she felt were heavy, and therefore stole out of doors direct and went to her father, who was always indulgent. How good and tender he was, never finding fault! If perhaps, as Rose was beginning to fear, it must be confessed that he was deficient in energy—a gentle accusation which the fondest partisan might allow—yet, to balance this, how good he was, how feeling, how tender! No one need be afraid to go to him. He was always ready to hear one's story, to forgive one's mistakes. Rose, who did not want to be catechised, stole across the lawn and sat down on the grass without a word. She did not care to meet anybody's look just at that moment. She had not cried; but the tears were so very near the surface, that any chance encounter of looks might have been more than she could bear.

Mr. Damerel did not speak all at once. He took time, the more cunningly to betray her; and then he entered upon one of his usual conversations, to which poor Rose gave but little heed. After a while her monosyllabic answers seemed to attract his curiosity all at once.

"You are not well," he said; "or sorry, is it? Sorry for poor Mrs. Wodehouse, who is going to lose her son?"

"Oh yes, papa! Poor old lady—she will be so lonely when he is away."

"She is not so very old," he said, amused; "not so old as I am, and I don't feel myself a Methuselah. It is very good of you to be so sympathizing, my dear."

"Oh, papa, who could help it?" said Rose, almost feeling as if her father would approve the shedding of those tears which made her eyes so hot and heavy. She plucked a handful of grass and played with it, her head held down and the large drops gathering; and her heart, poor child, for the moment, in the fulness of this first trouble, felt more heavy than her eyes.

"Yes, it is a pity for Mrs. Wodehouse," said Mr. Damerel, reflectively; "but, on the other hand, it would be very selfish to regret it for Edward. He has not a penny, poor fellow, and not much influence that I know of. He can only get his promotion by service, and in this point of view his friends ought to be glad he is going. Look across Ankermead, Rose; how soft the shadows are! the most delicate gray with silvery lights. If you were a little more ambitious as an artist, you might get your sketch-book and try that effect."

Rose smiled a wan little smile in answer to this invitation, and looking down upon the landscape, as he told her to do, saw nothing but a bluish-green and yellow mist through the prismatic medium of the big tear, which next moment, to her terror and misery, came down, a huge, unconcealable wet blot, upon her light summer dress. She was herself so struck by consternation at the sight that, instead of making any attempt to conceal it, she looked up at him, her lips falling apart, her eyes growing larger and larger with fright and wonder, half appealing to him to know what it could mean, half defying observation. Mr. Damerel saw that it was necessary to abandon his usual rule of indulgence.

"You are too sympathetic, my dear," he said. "If any one but me saw this they might say such feeling was too strong to be lavished on Mrs. Wodehouse. Don't let us hear any more of it. Have you finished 'Balaustion'? You have no book with you to-day."

"No, papa—I came out—the other way"—

"What does that mean? Not through the drawing-room, where you left it, and where your mother was? I think you were right, Rose," said Mr. Damerel, dropping back in his chair with his easy smile; "your mother has little patience with Mrs. Wodehouse's despairs and miseries. You had better keep your sympathy to yourself in her presence. Look here; I want this read aloud. My eyes ache; I was up late last night."

Rose took the book obediently, and read. She saw the white page and letters clear without any prismatic lights. Her tears were all driven away, forced back upon her heart as if by a strong wind. She read, as Milton's daughters might have read his Latin, if they did not understand it, as some people say—not missing a word nor seeing any meaning in one; going on as in a dream, with a consciousness of herself, and the scene, and her father's look, and not a notion what she was reading about. It was very good mental discipline, but so sharp that this poor soft child, utterly unused to it, not knowing why she should suddenly be subjected to such fierce repression, wretched and sick at heart, and sorry and ashamed, never forgot it all her life. She read thus for about an hour, till her father stopped her to make some notes upon the margin of the book; for he was one of those elegantly studious persons who weave themselves through the books they read, and leave volumes of notes on every possible subject behind them. He had been entering into every word, though Rose had not understood a syllable; and he smiled and discoursed to her about it, while she kept silent, terrified lest he should ask some question, which would betray her inattention. Rose had been learning smilingly, with happy bewilderment, for some months back, to consider herself an independent individual. She felt and realized it without any difficulty to-day. She stood quite alone in all that bright scene; apart from the real world and the ideal both—neither the lawn, nor the book, nor the landscape, nor her father's talk having power to move her; frightened at herself—still more frightened for him, and for the tone, half sarcastic, half reproving, which for the first time in her life she had heard in his voice; and without even the satisfaction of realizing the new sentiment which had come into her mind. She realized nothing except that sudden dismay had come over her, that it had been checked summarily; that her tears, driven back, were filling her head and her heart with confusing pain; that there was something wrong in the strange new emotion that was at work within her—and this without even the melancholy sweetness of knowing what it was.

Poor Rose in June! It was the first storm that had ever disturbed her perfect blossom. She began to get better after a while, as at her age it is easy to do, and gradually came out of her mist and was restored to partial consciousness. By the evening of that day she was nearly herself again, though much subdued, remembering that she had been very unhappy, as she might have remembered a very bad headache, with great content, yet wonder that it should be gone or almost gone. The cessation of the active pain gave her a kind of subdued happiness once more, as relief always does—which the heart never feels to be negative, but positive. What a thing ease is, after we are once conscious of having lost it even for an hour! This brought Rose's color back and her smile. All mental pain, I suppose, is spasmodic; and the first fit, when not too well defined nor hopeless in character, is often as brief as it is violent.

Rose got better; her mind accustomed itself to the shadow which for one short interval had covered it with blackness. She began to perceive that it did not fill all earth and heaven, as she had at first supposed.

CHAPTER V.

ROSE grew very much better, almost quite well, next day. There was still a little thrill about her of the pain past, but in the mean time nothing had yet happened, no blank had been made in the circle of neighbors; and though she was still as sorry as ever, she said to herself, for poor Mrs. Wodehouse (which was the only reason she had ever given to herself for that *serrement de cœur*), yet there were evident consolations in that poor lady's lot, if she could but see them. Edward would come back again; she would get letters from him; she would have him still, though he was away. She was his inalienably, whatever distance there might be between them. This seemed a strong argument to Rose in favor of a brighter view of the subject, though I do not think it would have assisted Mrs. Wodehouse; and, besides, there were still ten days, which—as a day is eternity to a child—was as good as a year at least to Rose. So she took comfort, and preened herself like a bird, and came again forth to the day in all her sweet bloom, her tears got rid of in the natural way, her eyes no longer hot and heavy. She scarcely observed even, or at least did not make any mental note of the fact, that she did not see Edward Wodehouse for some days thereafter. "How sorry I am to have missed them!" her mother said, on hearing that the young man and his mother had called in her absence; and Rose was sorry too, but honestly took the fact for an accident. During the ensuing days there was little doubt that an unusual amount of occupation poured upon her. She went with her father to town one morning to see the pictures in the exhibitions. Another day she was taken by the same delightful companion to the other side of the county to a garden party, which was the most beautiful vision of fine dresses and fine people Rose had ever seen. I cannot quite describe what the girl's feelings were while she was going through these unexpected pleasures. She liked them, and was pleased and flattered; but at the same time a kind of giddy sense of something being done to her which she could not make out,—some force being put upon her, she could not tell what, or for why,—was in her mind. For the first time in her life she was jealous and curious, suspecting some unseen motive, though she could not tell what it might be.

On the fourth day her father and mother both together took her with them to Mr. Incledon's, to see, they said, a new picture which he had just bought—a Perugino, or, it might be, an early Raphael. "He wants my opinion—and I want yours, Rose," said her father, flattering, as he always did, his favorite child.

"And Mr. Incledon wants hers, too," said Mrs. Damerel. "I don't know what has made him think you a judge, Rose."

"Oh! how can I give an opinion—what do I know?" said Rose, bewildered; but she was pleased, as what girl would not be pleased? To have her opinion prized was pleasant, even though she felt that it was a subject upon which she could pass no opinion. "I have never seen any but the Raphaels in the National Gallery," she said, with alarmed youthful conscientiousness, as they went along, "and what can I know?"

"You can tell him if you like it; and that will please him as much as if you were the first art critic in England," said the rector. These words gave Rose a little thrill of suspicion—for why should Mr. Incledon care for her opinion?—and perplexed her thoughts much as she walked up the leafy road to the gate of Whitton Park, which was Mr. Incledon's grand house. Her father expatiated upon the beauty of the place as they went in; her mother looked preoccupied and anxious; and Rose herself grew more and more suspicious, though she was surprised into some exclamations of pleasure at the beauty and greenness of the park.

"I wonder I have never been here before," she said; "how could it be? I thought we had been everywhere when we were children, the boys and I."

"Mr. Incledon did not care for children's visits," said her mother.

"And he was in the right, my dear. Children have no eye for beauty; what they want is space to tumble about in, and trees to climb. This lovely bit of woodland would be lost on boys and girls. Be thankful you did not see it when you were incapable of appreciating it, Rose."

"It is very odd, though," she said. "Do you think it is nice of Mr. Incledon to shut up so pretty a place from his neighbors—from his friends?—for, as we have always lived so near, we are his friends, I suppose."

"Undoubtedly," said the rector; but his wife said nothing. I do not think her directer mind cared for this way of influencing her daughter. She was anxious for the same object, but she would have attained it in a different way.

Here, however, Mr. Incledon himself appeared with as much demonstration of delight to see them as was compatible with the supposed accidental character of the visit. Mr. Incledon was one of those men of whom you feel infallibly certain that they must have been "good," even in their nurse's arms. He was slim and tall, and looked younger than he really was. He had a good expression, dark eyes, and his features, though not at all remarkable, were good enough to give him the general aspect of a handsome man. Whether he was strictly handsome or not was a frequent subject of discussion on the Green, where unpleasant things had been said about his chin and his eyebrows, but where the majority was distinctly in his favor. His face was long, his complexion rather dark, and his general appearance "interesting." Nobody that I know of had ever called him commonplace. He was interesting—a word which often stands high in the rank of descriptive adjectives. He was the sort of man of whom imaginative persons might suppose that he had been the hero of a story. Indeed, there were many theories on the subject; and ingenious observers, chiefly ladies, found a great many symptoms of this in his appearance and demeanor, and concluded that a man so well off and so well looking would not have remained unmarried so long had there not been some reason for it. But this phase of his existence was over, so far as his own will was concerned. If he had ever had any reason for remaining unmarried, that obstacle must have been removed; for he was now anxious to marry, and had fully made up his mind to do so at as early a date as possible. I do not know whether it could be truly said that he was what foolish young people call "very much in love" with Rose Damerel; but he had decided that she was the wife for him, and meant to spare neither pains nor patience in winning her. He had haunted the rectory for some time, with a readiness to accept all invitations which was entirely unlike his former habits; for up to the time when he had seen and made up his mind about Rose, Mr. Incledon had been almost a recluse, appearing little in the tranquil society of the Green, spending much of his time abroad, and when at home holding only a reserved and distant intercourse with his neighbors. He gave them a handsome heavy dinner two or three times a year, and accepted the solemn return which society requires; but no one at Dinglefield had seen more of his house than the reception-rooms, or of himself than those grave festivities exhibited. The change upon him now was marked enough to enlighten the most careless looker-on; and the Perugino, which they were invited to see, was in fact a pretence which the rector and his wife saw through very easily, to make them acquainted with his handsome house and all its advantages. He took them all over it, and showed the glory of it with mingled complacency and submission to their opinion. Rose had never been within its walls before. She had never sat down familiarly in rooms so splendid. The master of the house had given himself up to furniture and decorations as only a rich man can do; and the subdued grace of everything about them, the wealth of artistic ornament, the size and space which always impress people who are accustomed to small houses, had no inconsiderable effect, at least upon the ladies of the party. Mr. Damerel was not awed, but he enjoyed the largeness and the luxury with the satisfaction of a man who felt himself in his right sphere; and Mr. Incledon showed himself, as well as his house, at his best, and, conscious that he was doing so, looked, Mrs. Damerel thought, younger, handsomer, and more attractive than he had ever looked before. Rose felt it, too, vaguely. She felt that she was herself somehow the centre of all—the centre, perhaps, of a plot, the nature of which perplexed and confused her; but the plot was not yet sufficiently advanced to give her any strong sensation of discomfort or fear. All that it did up to the present moment was to convey that sense of importance and pleasant consciousness of being the first and most flatteringly considered, which is always sweet to youth. Thus they were all pleased, and, being pleased, became more and more pleasant to each other. Rose, I think, forgot poor Mrs. Wodehouse altogether for the moment, and was as gay as if she had never been sad.

The house was a handsome house, raised on a slightly higher elevation than the rectory, surrounded by a pretty though not very extensive park, and commanding the same landscape as that which it was the pride of the Damerels to possess from their windows. It was the same, but with a difference; or, rather, it was like a view of the same subject painted by a different artist, dashed in in bolder lines, with heavier massing of foliage, and one broad reach of the river giving a great centre of light and shadow, instead of the dreamy revelations here and there of the winding water as seen from the rectory. Rose gave an involuntary cry of delight when she was taken out to the green terrace before the house, and first saw the landscape from it, though she never would confess afterwards that she liked it half so well as the shadowy distance and softer, sweep of country visible from her old home. Mr. Incledon was as grateful to her for her admiration as if the Thames and the trees had been of his making and ventured to draw near confidentially and say how much he hoped she would like his Perugino—or, perhaps, Raphael. "You must give me your opinion frankly," he said.

"But I never saw any Raphaels except those in the National Gallery," said Rose, blushing with pleasure, and shamefacedness, and conscientious difficulty. It did not occur to the girl that her opinion could be thus gravely asked for by a man fully aware of its complete worthlessness as criticism. She thought he must have formed some mistaken idea of her knowledge or power. "And I don't—love them—

very much," she added, with a little hesitation and a deeper blush, feeling that his momentary good opinion of her must now perish forever.

"What does that mean?" said Mr. Incledon. He was walking on with her through, as she thought, an interminable vista of rooms, one opening into the other, towards the shrine in which he had placed his picture. "There is something more in it than meets the ear. It does not mean that you don't like them"—

"It means—that I love the photograph of the San Sisto, that papa gave me on my birthday," said Rose.

"Ah! I perceive; you are a young critic to judge so closely. We have nothing like that, have we? How I should like to show you the San Sisto picture! Photographs and engravings give no idea of the original."

"Oh, please don't say so!" said Rose, "for so many people never can see the original. I wish I might some time. The pictures in the National Gallery do not give me at all the same feeling; and, of course, never having seen but these, I cannot be a judge; indeed, I should not dare to say anything at all. Ah, ah!"

Rose stopped and put her hands together, as she suddenly perceived before her, hung upon a modest gray-green wall with no other ornament near, one of those very youthful, heavenly faces, surrounded by tints as softly bright as their own looks, which belong to that place and period in which Perugino taught and Raphael learned—an ineffable sweet ideal of holiness, tenderness, simplicity, and youth. The girl stood motionless, subdued by it, conscious of nothing but the picture. It was doubly framed by the doorway of the little room in which it kept court. Before even she entered that sacred chamber, the young worshipper was struck dumb with adoration. The doorway was hung with silken curtains of the same gray-green as the wall, and there was not visible, either in this soft surrounding framework, or in the picture itself, any impertinent accessory to distract the attention. The face so tenderly abstract, so heavenly human, looked at Rose as at the world, but with a deeper, stronger appeal; for was not Mary such a one as she? The girl could not explain the emotion which seized her. She felt disposed to kneel down, and she felt disposed to weep, but did neither; only stood there, with her lips apart, her eyes abstract yet wistful, like those in the picture; and her soft hands clasped and held unconsciously, with that dramatic instinct common to all emotion, somewhere near her heart.

"You *have* said something," said Mr. Incledon, softly, in her ear, "more eloquent than I ever heard before. I am satisfied that it is a Raphael now."

"Why?" said Rose, awakening with great surprise out of her momentary trance, and shrinking back, her face covered with blushes, to let the others pass who were behind. He did not answer her except by a look, which troubled the poor girl mightily, suddenly revealing to her the meaning of it all. When the rest of the party went into the room, Rose shrank behind her mother, cowed and ashamed, and instead of looking at the picture, stole aside to the window and looked out mechanically to conceal her troubled countenance. As it happened, the first spot on which her eye fell was the little cottage at Ankermead, upon which just the other evening she had looked with Edward Wodehouse. All he said came back to her, and the evening scene in which he said it, and the soft, indescribable happiness and sweetness that had dropped upon her like the falling dew. Rose had not time to make any question with herself as to what it meant; but her heart jumped up in her bosom and began to beat, and a sudden, momentary perception of how it all was flashed over her. Such gleams of consciousness come and go when the soul is making its first experiences of life. For one second she seemed to see everything clearly as a landscape is seen when the sun suddenly breaks out; and then the light disappeared, and the clouds re-descended, and all was blurred again. Nevertheless, this strange, momentary revelation agitated Rose almost more than anything that had ever happened to her before; and everything that was said after it came to her with a muffled sound, as we hear voices in a dream. A longing to get home and to be able to think took possession of her. This seemed for the moment the thing she most wanted in the world.

"If ever I have a wife," Mr. Incledon said, some time after, "this shall be her boudoir. I have always intended so; unless, indeed, she is perverse as my mother was, who disliked this side of the house altogether, and chose rooms which looked out on nothing but the park and the trees."

"I hope, as everything is ready for her, the lady will soon appear," said Mrs. Damerel; while poor little Rose suddenly felt her heart stop in its beating, and flutter and grow faint.

"Ah!" said Incledon, shaking his head, "it is easier to gild the cage than to secure the bird."

How glad she was when they were out again in the open air, walking home! How delightful it was to be going home, to get off this dangerous ground, to feel that there was a safe corner to fly to! Nobody said anything to her, fortunately for Rose, but let her walk off her excitement and the flutter of terror and dismay which had come over her. "Easier to gild the cage than to secure the bird." The poor little bird felt already as if she had been caught in some snare; as if the fowler had got his hand upon her, and all her flutterings would be of no avail. How little she had thought that this was what was meant by their flattering eagerness to have her opinion about the Perugino! She kept close to her mother till they got safely out of the park, for Mr. Incledon attended them as far as the gates, and Rose was so much startled that she did not feel safe near him. It seemed to her that the plot must be brought to perfection at once, and that there was no escape except in keeping as far off as possible. She resolved to herself as she went along that she would never approach him if she could help it, or let him speak to her. Her sensations were something like those with which a startled hare might, I suppose, contemplate from beneath her couch of fern the huntsman gathering the hounds which were to run her down. Rose had no sense of satisfaction such as an older woman might have felt, in the love of so important a personage as Mr. Incledon. She was neither flattered nor tempted by the thought of all the good things she might have at her disposal as his wife—his beautiful house, his wealth, his consequence, even his Perugino, though that had drawn the very heart out of her breast —none of these things moved her. She was neither proud of his choice, nor dazzled by his wealth. She was simply frightened, neither more nor less—dead frightened, and eager to escape forever out of his way.

It was now afternoon, the most languid hour of the day, and the village roads were very hot, blazing, and dusty, after the soft shade of Whitton Park. Mr. Damerel, who was not much of a pedestrian, and hated dust, and abhorred all the irritations and weariness of excessive heat, came along somewhat slowly, skirting the houses to get every scrap of shade which was possible. They were thus quite close to a row of cottages when Mr. Nolan came out from the door of one so suddenly as almost to stumble over his rector.

"Just like a shot from a cannon is an Irishman's exit from a visit," said Mr. Damerel, peevishly, though playfully. "Nolan, you salamander, you who never feel the heat, you may at least have some pity upon me."

"You are the very man I want," said the curate, whose brow was clouded with care. "The poor creature's dying. You'll go and say a word to her? I was going to your house, wondering would I find ye? and lo! Providence puts ye here."

"I hope I shall feel as much obliged to Providence as you do," said the rector still more peevishly. "What is it? Who is it? What do you want?"

"Sure it's only a poor creature dying—nothing to speak about in this dreary world" said good Mr. Nolan; "but she has a fancy to see you. I have done all I could to pacify her; but she says she knew you in her better days."

"It is old Susan Aikin," said Mrs. Damerel, in answer to her husband's inquiring look. "She has always wanted to see you; but what good could you do her? and she has had a bad fever, and it is a miserable place."

"Not that you'll think twice of that," said Nolan hurriedly, "when it's to give a bit of comfort to a dying creature that longs to see you;" though indeed it would puzzle the world to tell why, he added in his heart.

"Certainly not," said the rector—a quantity of fine wrinkles, unseen on ordinary occasions, suddenly appearing like a net-work on his forehead. His voice took a slightly querulous tone, in spite of the readiness with which he replied. "You need not wait," he said, turning to his wife and daughter. "Go on gently, and perhaps I may overtake you if it is nothing important. What is it, Nolan; a case of troubled conscience? Something on her mind?"

"Nothing but a dyin' fancy," said Mr. Nolan. "She's harped on it these three days. No, she's a good soul enough; there's no story to tell; and all her duties done, and life closing as it ought. It's but a whim; but they will all take it as a great favor," said the curate, seeing that his superior officer looked very much in the mind to turn and fly.

"A whim," he said, querulously. "You know I am not careless of other people's feelings—far from it, I hope; but my own organization is peculiar, and to undergo this misery for a whim—you said a whim"—

"But the creature's dying!"

"Pah! what has dying to do with it? Death is a natural accident. It is not meritorious to die, or a thing to which every other interest should yield and bow. But, never mind," the rector added, after this little outbreak; "it is not your fault—come, I'll go."

Rose and her mother had lingered to hear the end of the discussion; and just as the rector yielded thus, and, putting as good a grace as possible on the unwillingly performed duty, entered, led by Mr. Nolan, the poor little cottage, the ladies were joined by Mrs. Wodehouse and her son, who had hurried up at sight of them. Mrs. Wodehouse had that reserved and solemn air which is usual to ladies who are somewhat out of temper with their friends. She was offended, and she meant to show it. She said "Good morning" to Mrs. Damerel, instead of "How do you do?" and spoke with melancholy grandeur of the weather, and the extreme heat, and how a thunderstorm must be on its way. They stood talking on these interesting topics, while Rose and Edward found themselves together. It seemed to Rose as if she was seeing him for the first time after a long absence or some great event. The color rushed to her face in an overwhelming flood, and a tide of emotions as warm, as tumultuous, as bewildering, rushed into her heart. She scarcely ventured to lift her eyes when she spoke to him. It seemed to her that she understood now every glance he gave her, every tone of his voice.

"I almost feared we were not to meet again," he said hurriedly; "and these last days run through one's fingers so fast. Are you going out to-night?"

"I do not think so," said Rose, half afraid to pledge herself, and still more afraid lest her mother should hear and interpose, saying, "Yes, they were engaged."

"Then let me come to-night. I have only four days more. You will not refuse to bid a poor sailor good-by, Miss Damerel? You will not let them shut me out to-night?"

"No one can wish to shut you out," said Rose, raising her eyes to his face for one brief second.

I do not think Edward Wodehouse was so handsome as Mr. Incledon. His manners were not nearly so perfect; he could not have stood comparison with him in any respect except youth, in which he had the better of his rival; but oh, how different he seemed to Rose! She could not look full at him; only cast a momentary glance at his honest, eager eyes; his face, which glowed and shone with meaning. And now she knew what the meaning was.

"So long as *you* don't!" he said, eagerly, yet below his breath; and just at this moment Mrs. Damerel put forth her hand and took her daughter by the arm.

"We have had a long walk, and I am tired," she said. "We have been to Whitton to see a new picture, and Mr. Incledon has so many beautiful things. Come, Rose. Mr. Wodehouse, I hope we shall see you before you go away."

"Oh, yes, I hope so," the young sailor faltered, feeling himself suddenly cast down from heaven to earth. He said nothing to her about that evening, but I suppose Mrs. Damerel's ears were quick enough to hear the important appointment that had been made.

"My dear Rose, girls do not give invitations to young men, nor make appointments with them, generally, in that way."

"I, mamma?"

"Don't be frightened. I am not blaming you. It was merely an accident; but, my dear, it was not the right kind of thing to do."

"Must I not speak to Mr. Wodehouse?" she asked, half tremblingly, half (as she meant it) satirically. But poor Rose's little effusion of (what she intended for) gall took no effect whatever. Mrs. Damerel did not perceive that any satire was meant.

"Oh, you may speak to him! You may bid him good-by, certainly; but I—your papa—in short, we have heard something of Mr. Wodehouse which—we do not quite like. I do not wish for any more intimacy with them, especially just now."

"Do you mean you have heard some harm of him?" said Rose, opening her eyes with a sudden start.

"Well, perhaps not any harm; I cannot quite tell what it was; but something which made your papa decide—in short, I don't want to take too much notice of the Wodehouses as a family. They do not suit your papa."

Rose walked on with her mother to the rectory gate, silent, with her heart swelling full. She did not believe that her father had anything to do with it. It was not he who was to blame, whatever Mrs. Damerel might say.

CHAPTER VI.

NATURE took sides against Love on that evening, and made Mrs. Damerel's warning unnecessary, and all the anticipations of the young persons of no avail. Instead of the evening stroll about the darkling garden which Wodehouse at least had proposed to himself, the party were shut up in the drawing-room by the sudden outbreak of that expected thunderstorm on which Mrs. Wodehouse and Mrs. Damerel had discussed so earnestly. The ladies had both felt that it must come, and the young sailor, I suppose, ought to have been more clearly aware of what was impending; but there are, no doubt, states of the mind which make a man totally indifferent to, and unobservant of, the changes of the atmosphere. Anyhow, though he arrived in the sweet beginning of the twilight, when all was still, poor Edward had not only to stay in-doors, but to take a seat next to Mrs. Damerel in the drawing-room; while Rose, who was somewhat nervous about the thunder, retired into a dark corner to which he dared not follow her boldly under the very eyes of her father and her mother. He did what he could, poor fellow: he tried very hard to persuade her to come to the other end of the room and watch the storm which was raging gloriously on the plain below, lighting up the whole landscape in sudden, brilliant gleams; for one of the windows had been left uncurtained and Mr. Damerel himself placed his chair within reach of it to enjoy the wonderful spectacle. Rose at one time longed so much to venture that her desire overmastered her fears; but the rector, who was somewhat fretful that evening, presumably on account of the storm, which affected his fine sensibilities, sent her away hurriedly. "No, no, Rose—what have you to do with storms?" he said; "go back to your mother." When she obeyed, there was silence in the room; and though the elders did not care very much for it, I think the sharp disappointment of these two—a pang, perhaps, more keen and delicate than anything we can feel when the first freshness of youth is over—made itself spiritually felt somehow in the atmosphere of the place.

"Roses have nothing to do out of the rose garden," said Mr. Damerel, with an attempt to overcome his own fretfulness, and perhaps a compunction over the suffering he caused. He was not in a humor for talking, and when this was the case he seldom gave himself the trouble to talk; but some covert feeling or other made him willing to attempt a diversion, for the moment at least. "I wish people had a more general conception of the fitness of things. Your namesakes out-of-doors take no pleasure in the storm. Poor roses, how it will batter and beat them down, and strew their poor helpless petals about!"

"I do not find fault with Rose for being timid," said her mother; "but your craze about her name is fantastic, Herbert. She will have a good many storms to brave which she cannot escape from if she is to do her duty in life."

"Then I hope she will not do her duty," said the rector; "don't, my Rose in June. I had rather see you sweet and fresh, with your rose heart unruffled, than draggled and battered with the rain. I'll take the moral risk upon my own head."

Mrs. Damerel uttered an impatient little exclamation under her breath. She turned to Wodehouse with an arbitrary and sudden change of the subject. "Do you expect to be long away?" she said.

"Two years at the very least," said the young man, piteously, looking at her with such imploring eyes that she felt his look, though her own eyes were fixed upon her work, and neither could nor would see. She felt it; and as she was but a woman, though stern in purpose, she winced a little and was sorry for him, though she would not help him. Her voice softened as she replied,—

"I am very sorry for your poor mother. How she will miss you! We must do our best to keep her cheerful while you are away."

"The storm is going off," said the rector; "did you ever remark, Wodehouse, how seldom we have a complete thunderstorm to ourselves here? There have been three going on to-night: one towards London, one northwards, the other east. We never have more than the tail of a storm, which is somewhat humbling when you come to think of it. I suppose it has something to do with the *lie* of the ground as you call it—eh?"

Edward answered something, he did not know what, while his opponent regarded him with amused observation. Now that the matter was tolerably safe in his own hands, Mr. Damerel was not without a certain enjoyment in the study of character thus afforded him. It was to him like what I suppose vivisection is to an enterprising physiologist. He had just enough realization of the pain he was inflicting to give interest to the throbbing nerves upon which he experimented. He was not old enough to have quite forgotten some few pangs of a similar kind which he had experienced in his day; but he was old enough to regard the recollection with some degree of amusement and a sense of the absolute folly of the whole which neutralized that sense of pain. He liked, rather, to hold the young man in talk about scientific facts, while he knew that the young man was longing to escape, and watching, with dismay and despair, every hope disappearing of another kind of conversation which seemed like the balance of life and death to the foolish youth. Mr. Damerel saw all these symptoms of torture, and his sense of humor was tickled. He was almost sorry when at length, the rain still continuing to fall in torrents and the storm roaring and groaning in the distance, young Wodehouse rose to go away. "I will not give you my blessing again," he said, smiling, "as I was rash enough to do before; for I dare say we shall meet again, one way or another, before you go away."

"Oh, I shall call when the last moment, the absolute good-by, comes!" said poor Edward, trying to smile.

Rose put out a timid little hand to him, rising from her chair when he came up to her. She had grown bewildered again, and disconcerted, and had fallen far from the light and illumination which had flashed over her in the afternoon. The storm had frightened her: something malign seemed in the air; and she was disappointed and mortified, she scarcely could have told why. Was this to be the end of the evening to which they had both looked forward? Alas! such clouds will drop over even the brightest skies. I think both of the young people could have wept with sheer misery, disappointment, and despite, when they realized that it was over, and could not now be mended, whatever might happen. He went home, and she stole up to her room, enveloped by the mists of a suppressed excitement which seemed to wrap them round and round, and afforded no way of escape.

That, however, was the last bright day known in the rectory for a very long time. The rector had not been quite himself that night. His very pleasure in the torture of the poor young lovers was perhaps a sign that the fine organization upon which he prided himself was somehow out of gear. I do not believe, though many people were of that opinion, that his hurried visit to the poor woman who was dying of fever was the reason why Mr. Damerel took the fever, and of all that followed. He could not have fallen ill so immediately if poor Susan Aikin's death-chamber had been the cause of his malady. Next day he was ill, feverish, and wretched, and was reported to have a bad cold. The next after that the village and all the houses on the Green were struck dumb by the information that the rector had caught the same fever of which Susan Aikin died. The news caused such a sensation as few warnings of mortality produce. The whole neighborhood was hushed and held its breath, and felt a shiver of dismay run through it. It was not because Mr. Damerel was deeply beloved. Mr. Nolan, for example, was infinitely more friendly and dear to the population generally; yet had he encountered the same fate people would have grieved, but would not have been surprised. But the rector! that he should fall under such a disease—that the plague which is born of squalor, and dirt, and ill nourishment, and bad air should seize upon him, the very impersonation of everything that was opposite and antagonistic to those causes which brought it forth!—this confused everybody, great and small. Comfortable people shuddered, asking themselves who was safe? and began to think of the drainage of their houses, and to ask whether any one knew if the rectory was quite right in that respect. There was an anxious little pause of fright in the place, every one wondering whether it was likely to prove an epidemic, and neighbor inquiring of neighbor each time they met whether "more cases" had occurred; but this phase passed over, and the general security came back. The disease must "take its course," the doctor said, and nothing could be prognosticated at so early a stage. The patient was still in middle age, of unbroken constitution, and had everything in his favor—good air, good nursing, good means—so that nothing need be spared. With such words as these the anxieties of the neighborhood were relieved—something unwillingly it must be allowed, for the world is very *exigeant* in this as in many other respects, and, when it is interested in an illness, likes it to run a rapid course, and come to an issue one way or other without delay. It was therefore with reluctance that the Green permitted itself to be convinced that no "change" could be looked for in the rector's illness for some time to come. Weeks even might be consumed ere the climax, the crisis, the real dramatic point at which the patient's fate would be concluded, should come. This chilling fact composed the mind of the neighborhood, and stilled it back into the calm of indifference after a while. I am not sure now that there was not a little adverse feeling towards the rector, in that he left everybody in suspense, and having, as it were, invited the world to behold the always interesting spectacle of a dangerous illness, put off from week to week the *dénouement*. Such a barbarous suggestion would have been repulsed with scorn and horror had it been put into words, but that was the feeling in most people's hearts.

In-doors, however, Mr. Damerel's illness was a very terrible matter, and affected every member of the household. Mrs. Damerel gave up everything to nurse him. There was no hesitation with her as to whether she should or should not postpone her family and cares to her husband. From the moment that the dreadful word "fever" crossed the doctor's lips she put aside the house and the school-room and every other interest, and took her place by the sick-bed. I do not know if any foreboding was in her mind from the first, but she never paused to think. She went to the children and spoke to them, appealing to their honor and affection. She gave Dick and Patty permission to roam as they liked, and to enjoy perfect immunity from lessons and routine, so long as they would be quiet in-doors, and respect the stillness that was necessary in the house; and to Agatha she gave the charge of the infants, exacting quiet only, nothing but quiet. "The house must be kept quiet," she said to them all imperatively. "The child who makes a noise I shall think no child of mine. Your papa's life may depend upon it. It will be Rose's part to see that you all do what I tell you. No noise! that is the chief thing. There must be no noise!"

The children all promised very solemnly, and even closed round her with great eyes uplifted to ask in hushed tones of awe, as if he had been dead, how papa was? The house altogether was strangely subdued all at once, as if the illness had already lasted for weeks. The drawing-room became a shut-up, uninhabited place, where Rose only entered now and then to answer the inquiries of some anxious parishioners not too frightened to come and ask how the rector was. The tide of life, of interest, of occupation, all flowed towards the sick-room—everything centred in it. After a few days it would have seemed as unnatural to Rose to have gone out to the lawn as it was at first to sit in the little anteroom, into which her father's room opened, waiting to receive her mother's commissions, to do anything she might want of her. A few days sufficed to make established habits of all these new circumstances of life. Mr. Damerel was not a bad patient. He was a little angry and annoyed when he found what his illness was, taking it for granted, as so many people did, that he had taken it from Susan Aikin. "I wish Providence had directed me anywhere else than to that cottage door at that particular moment," he said, half ruefully, half indignantly, "and put me in the way of that fanatic Nolan, who can stand everything. I knew my constitution was very different. Never mind, it was not *your* fault, Martha; and he is a good fellow. I must try to push him on. I will write to the bishop about him when I get well."

These were heavenly dispositions, as the reader will perceive. He was a very good patient, grateful to his nurses, cheerful in his demeanor, making the best of the long struggle he had embarked upon—indeed, few people could have rallied more bravely from the first shock and discouragement, or composed themselves more courageously to fill the first position which was forced upon him, and discharge all its duties, such as they were. His illness came on not violently, but in the leisurely, quiet way which so often distinguishes a disease which is meant to last long. He was ill, but not very ill, on the fourth day, descending into depths of it, but going very quietly, and retaining his self-command and cheerfulness. This particular day, on which he was a little worse than he had been before, was mild and rainy and warm, very unlike the wonderful blaze of summer which had preceded it. Rose sat by the open window of the little anteroom, which was now her general position. The rain fell softly outside with a subdued, perpetual sound, pattering upon the leaves. The whole atmosphere was full of this soft patter. The door of the sick-room was ajar, and now and then Rose heard her father move in the restlessness of his illness, or utter a low little moan of suffering, or speak to Mrs. Damerel, who was with him. Everything was hushed down-stairs; and the subdued stirring of the rain outside, and the sounds of the sick-room within, were all that Rose could hear. She had a book in her hand, and read now and then; but she had come for the first time to that point in life when one's own musings are as interesting as any story, and often the book dropped on her lap, and she did nothing but think. She thought it was thinking, but I fancy that dreaming was more like it. Poor Rose! her dreaming was run through by sombre threads, and there was one shadow of wondering doubt and suspicion mingled in it. As she sat thus, one of the maids came softly to the door to say that Mrs. Wodehouse and her son were in the drawing-room, and would she tell Mrs. Damerel? Rose's heart gave a sudden leap; she hesitated a moment whether she should not run down without saying anything to her mother, as it was she, up to this moment, who had answered all inquiries; but the habit of dependence prevailed over this one eager throb of nature. She stole into the sick-room under shade of the curtains, and gave her message. The answer had invariably been, "Go you, Rose, and tell them I am very sorry, but I cannot leave your papa." She expected to hear the same words again, and stood, half-turned to the door, ready, when authorized, to rush down-stairs, with her heart already throbbing, and nature preparing in her for a crisis.

"What is it?" said the patient, drowsily.

"It is Edward Wodehouse come to say good-by," answered his wife. "Herbert, can you do without me for a moment? I ought to go."

"Yes: go, go; Rose will stay with me instead," said Mr. Damerel. He put out his hot hand and drew the girl towards him, who almost resisted, so stupefied was she. "Do not be long, Martha," he said to his wife; and before Rose could realize what had happened she found herself in her mother's chair, seated in the shaded stillness near the sick-bed, while Mrs. Damerel's step going softly along the passage outside testified to the bewildering fact that it was she who was to receive the visitors. It was so sudden, so totally different from her expectations, so cruel a disappointment to her, that the girl sat motionless, struck dumb, counting the soft fall of her mother's steps, in the stupor that fell upon her. Her father said something, but she had not the heart to answer. It seemed incredible, impossible. After ten minutes or so, which seemed to Rose so many hours, during which she continued to sit dumb, listening to her father's stirrings in his restless bed and the pattering of the rain, the same maid came to the door again and handed in a little scrap of paper folded like a note. She opened it mechanically. It was from Mrs. Wodehouse. "Dear Rose, dearest Rose, come and bid my boy good-by, if it is only for a moment," it said. She put it down on the table, and rose up and looked at her father. "If only for a moment,"—he was not so ill that any harm could happen to him if he were left for a moment. He did not look ill at all, as he lay there with his eyes closed. Was he asleep?—and surely, surely for that moment she might go!

While she looked at him, her heart beating wildly, and something singing and throbbing in her ears, he opened his eyes. "What is it?" he said.

"It is—oh, papa I may I go for one moment—only for a moment—I should come back directly; to bid—poor—Mr. Wodehouse good-by?"

"What, could ye not watch with me one hour?" said the rector, with perhaps unintentional profaneness, smiling at her a smile which seemed to make Rose wild. He put out his hand again and took hers. "Never mind poor Mr. Wodehouse," he said; "he will get on very well without you. Stay with me, my Rose in June; to see you thus does me good."

"I should only stay one moment." Her heart beat so that it almost stifled her voice.

"No, my darling," he said, coaxingly; "stay with me."

And he held her hand fast. Rose stood gazing at him with a kind of desperation till he closed his eyes again, holding her tightly by the wrist. I think even then she made a little movement to get free—a movement balked by the closer clasping of his feverish fingers. Then she sat down suddenly on her mother's chair. The pulsations were in her ears like great roars of sound coming and going. "Very well, papa," she said, with a stifled voice.

I do not know how long it was before she heard steps below, for her senses were preternaturally quickened—and then the sound of the hall door closed, and then the rain again, as if nothing had happened. What had happened? Nothing, indeed, except that Mrs. Damerel herself had seen the visitors, which was a great compliment to them, as she never left her husband's side. By and by her soft steps came back again, approaching gradually up the stairs and the long corridor. The sound of them fell upon Rose's heart—was it all over then? ended forever? Then her mother came in, calm and composed, and relieved her. She did not even look at Rose, as if there were anything out of the ordinary in this very simple proceeding. She told her husband quietly that she had said good-by to young Wodehouse; that he was going early next morning; that she was very sorry for his poor mother. "Yes, my dear; but if mothers were always to be considered, sons would never do anything. Mayn't I have something to drink?" said the patient; and thus the subject was dismissed at once and forever.

"Go and see if Mary has made some fresh lemonade," said Mrs. Damerel. Rose obeyed mechanically. The pulses were still beating so that her blood seemed like the tide at sea beating upon a broad beach, echoing hollow and wild in huge rolling waves. She went down-stairs like one in a dream and got the lemonade and carried it back again, hearing her own steps as she had heard her mother's. When this piece of business was over, and Rose found herself again in the little anteroom, all alone, with nothing but the sound of the rain to fill up the silence, and the great waves of sound in her ears beginning to die into moans and dreary sobbing echoes, what can I say of her feelings? Was it possible that all was over and ended—that she would never more see him again— that he was gone without even a good-by? It was not only incredible to her, but it was intolerable; must she bear it? She could not bear it; yet she must. She stood at the window and looked out, and the bluish-gray world and the falling rain looked in at Rose, and no other sound came to console the aching in her heart. He was gone, and there was no hope that he would come back; and she could not, dared not, go to him. The evening went on while she sat in this train of excited feelings, wondering whether the anguish in her heart would not call for an answer somehow, and unable to believe that neither God nor man would interfere. When it was dark she broke forth from all control, and left her post, as she could not do when leaving it was of any use: but there is a point at which the intolerable cannot be borne any longer. She put a blue waterproof cloak on her, and went out into the rain and the dark; but what was poor Rose to do, even when her pain became past bearing? She strayed round the dark lawn, and looked, but in vain, for the lights of the cottage at Ankermead; and then she ventured to the gate, and stood there looking out, helpless and wistful. But no good angel whispered to Edward Wodehouse, heart-sore and wounded, what poor little watcher there was looking helplessly, piteously out upon the little gulf of distance which separated them as much as continents and oceans could have done. He was packing for his early journey, and she, poor maiden soul, could not go to him, nor could the cry of her heart reach him. When she had waited there a while, she went in again speechless and heart-broken, feeling indeed that all was over, and that neither light nor happiness would ever return to her more.

Poor child! I don't think it occurred to her to blame those who had done it, or even to ask herself whether they knew what they were doing. Perhaps she did not believe that they had done it willingly. I do not think she asked herself any question on the subject. She had to bear it, and she could not bear it. Her mind was capable of little more.

CHAPTER VII.

"It does not seem possible," said the rector, slowly; "and yet somehow I cannot help thinking sometimes that I must be going to die."

"Herbert!"

"It is very curious—very curious—my reason tells me so, not feeling. I myself am just what I always was; but I think the symptoms are against me, and I see it in Marsden's looks. Doesn't he say so to you?"

"Dear," said Mrs. Damerel, with a trembling voice, "he does not conceal from me that it is very serious; but oh, Herbert, how often have we seen even the children at death's door, and yet brought back!"

"At death's door," he said reflectively; "yes, that's a good expression—at the door of something unknown. Somehow it does not seem possible. One can believe it for others, not for one's self. The idea is very strange."

Mrs. Damerel was a good, religious woman; and her husband was a clergyman. She did not feel that this was how he ought to speak at such a moment, and the thought wrung her heart. "Dearest," she said, growing more tender in her grief and pity, "it is a thing we must all think of one time or another; and to you, who have served God faithfully, it must be something else than 'strange.'"

"What else?" he said, looking up at her. "I might say confusing, bewildering. To think that I am going I know not where, with no certainty of feeling that I shall ever know anything about it; that I am no longer a free agent, but helpless, like a leaf blown into a corner by the wind—I who for very nearly fifty years have had a voice in all that was done to me. My dear, I don't know that I ever realized before how strange it was."

"But—you are—happy, Herbert?" she said, in a low, imploring voice.

"Happy, am I? I don't know—why should I be happy? I know what I am leaving, but I don't know what I am going to. I don't know anything about it. Something is going to happen to me, of which I have not the least conception what it is. I am not afraid, my dear, if that is what you mean," he said, after a momentary pause.

This conversation took place weeks after the departure of Edward Wodehouse and the end of that first flowery chapter of Rose's life. Her parents had not thought very much of her feelings, being concerned with much weightier matters. It had been a very long, lingering illness, not so violent as some fevers, but less hopeful; the crisis was over, but the patient did not mend. He was dying, and his wife knew it; and, though no one as yet had made the solemn announcement to him, he had found it out. He was very weak; but his mind was not at all impaired, and he could talk, with only a pause now and then for breath, as calmly as ever. It was a curious spectacle. He was gathering his cloak round him like Cæsar, but with sensations less satisfied and consciously heroic. Mr. Damerel was not a man to be indifferent to the necessity of dying fitly, with dignity and grace, but he had confidence in himself that nothing would disturb the folds of his robes at that supreme moment; he knew that no spiritual dread or cowardice would impair his fortitude; it was not necessary for him to make any effort to meet with dignity the unknown which was approaching; and his mind was at leisure to survey the strange, unexpected situation in which he found himself—going to die, without knowing what dying was, or how it would affect him, or where it would place him. I do not know, though he was a clergyman, that there was anything religious in the organization of his mind, and he had never come under any of those vivid influences which make men religious—or, at least, which make them fervent religionists—whatever may be the constitution of their mind. Mr. Damerel was no sceptic. He believed what he had been taught, and what he had taught in turn to others. His mind was not doctrinal or dogmatic, any more than it was devout; but he believed in the broad truths of Christianity, in some sort of a heaven, and some sort of a hell. These beliefs, however, had no effect upon his present state of feeling. He was not afraid of the hereafter; but his mind was bewildered and confounded by the contemplation of something close at hand which he did not know, and could not know so long as he retained consciousness of this only world with which he was acquainted. He was absorbed by the contemplation of this mystery. He was not thinking of his sins, nor of reward, nor of punishment, nor of rest from his labors (which had not been many). In short, he did not consider the great change that was about to take place upon him from a religious point of view at all, but rather from one which was at once natural and philosophical. I should not like to blame him for this, as, perhaps, some people will do. When we have lost much that made life sweet; when our friends, our children, have gone before us into the unseen country; then, indeed, the heart learns many longings for that world in which alone there can be reunion and explanation of life's sore and weary mysteries. But this was not Mr. Damerel's case. There was no one waiting for him at the golden gates; except perhaps, those whom he had long forgotten, and who had gone out of his life. He was departing alone, the first of his generation; curious and solitary, not knowing where he was going. To God's presence; ah yes! but what did that mean?

"All the same, my dear," he said, cheerfully, rousing himself, "we must not make ourselves wretched about it. A thing that happens to every man cannot be so very bad; and, in the mean time, we must make the best of it. I ought to have thought of it, perhaps, more than I have done."

"Oh, Herbert! God is very merciful," said his wife, who was crying softly by his side.

"Yes, yes, that is quite true; but that is not what I was thinking of. I ought to have thought of what would follow in case of this happening which is about to happen. I ought to have tried to save; out how could I have saved out of the little pittance we had?"

"Dear, don't think of such things now."

"But I must think upon them. I have never had any extravagant tastes, and we have always lived very quietly; but I fear you will find a difference. What a blessed thing that you are the sort of woman you are! The struggle will not fall so heavily upon you as upon most people. Incledon, of course, will marry Rose"—

"Oh, Herbert! what does all this matter? Do not think of it. I would so much rather hear you speak of yourself."

"There is nothing to say about myself; and, perhaps, the less one thinks, in the circumstances, the better; it is a curious position to be in—that is all that one can say. Yes, Incledon will marry Rose; he will make her a very good husband. Do not let it be put off from any regard to me. He will be a great help to you; and you may trust him, I should think, to settle about the boys. Lay as much upon him as you can; he is quite able to bear it. If one had foreseen this, you know, there are many things that one might have done; but—curious!" said the rector, with a smile, "I can't believe in it, even now."

"Oh, Herbert, it is never too late for God! Perhaps your feeling is the right one. If He would but give you back to us now!"

"No, no; don't think there is anything prophetic in my feelings, my dear. You may be sure every man is like me, more or less," said Mr. Damerel. "I know we must all die; only it is impossible in respect to one's self; I am myself, you perceive, just as much as ever; and yet to-morrow, perhaps, or next day—there's the wonder. It makes one feel giddy now and then. About the boys: I have always felt that one time or other we should have to decide something for the boys. Leave it to Incledon; he is a practical man, and will know what to advise."

"Dear Herbert, if you can talk of it—oh, how much better it would be to tell me what *you* wish, that I might be guided by your own feeling, than to refer me to any one else!" said Mrs. Damerel, crying, kissing his hand, and gazing with wet eyes into his calm face.

"Oh, talk; yes, I can talk, but for a little catching of the breath, the same as ever, I think; but the boys are a troublesome subject. Leave it to Incledon; he knows all about that sort of thing. I think now, perhaps, that I might sleep."

And then the curtains were dropped, the watcher retired a little out of sight, and everything was subdued into absolute stillness. Mrs. Damerel sat down noiselessly in the background, and covered her face with her hands, and wept silent tears, few and bitter. She had felt him to be hard upon her many a day; she had seen what was wanting in him; but he was her husband, the first love of her youth, and her heart was rent asunder by this separation. She had enough to think of besides, had she been able; she had poverty to face, and to bring up her children as best she could in a world which henceforward would not be kind and soft to them as it had been hitherto. Her soul was heavy with a consciousness of all that was before her; but, in the mean time, she had room for no distinct feeling except one—that her husband, her love, was going to be taken from her. This tremendous parting, rending asunder of two lives that had been one, was more than enough to fill all her mind; she had room for nothing more.

And he slept, or thought he slept, floating out of the vague pain and wonder of his waking thoughts into strange, vague visions, dimmer still, and then back again to the fancies which were waking and not sleeping. There was a dim impression of painfulness in them, rather than pain itself; wonder, curiosity, and that strange sense of an absolute blank which makes the soul giddy and the brain swim. Sometimes his mind seemed to himself to wander, and he got astray somehow, and felt himself sinking in an unfathomable sea, or striving to make his way through some blackness of night, some thorny wood in which there was no path. I suppose he was asleep then; but even he himself scarcely knew.

When he woke it was evening, and the lamp, carefully shaded, had been lit at the other end of the room. He liked the light; and, when he stirred and spoke, the watchers made haste to draw back the curtains. The serene evening sky, full of soft tints of reflection from the sunset, with breaks of daffodil light melting into ineffable soft greenness and blueness, shone in through the uncurtained window which he liked to have left so, that he might see the sky. Rose and her mother were close by the bright circle made by the lamp, one of them preparing some drink for him, the other opening a new bottle of medicine which had just been sent. Though it was all so familiar to him, the fact that he was to go away so soon seemed to throw a strangeness over everything, and gave a bewildering novelty even to the figures he knew so well.

"More of Marsden's stuff," he said, with a low laugh; and his own voice sounded far off to him, as he lay looking at that strange little picture—a distant view of the two women against the light, with the sky and the window behind; somebody's wife and daughter—his own—his very Rose, and she who had been his companion since his youth. Strange that he should look at them so quietly, almost with an amused sense of novelty, without any tragic feeling or even pain to speak of, in the thought that he was going away shortly and would see them no more. He fell to thinking of a thousand things as he lay there watching them, yet not watching them. Not the things, perhaps, that a dying man ought to think of; little nothings, chance words that he had forgotten for years, lines of poetry, somehow connected with his present condition, though he did not remember the links of connection. "The casement slowly grows, a glittering square," he said to himself, and made an effort to think whence the line came, and why it should have at this moment thrust itself into his mind. Then he fell altogether into a poetic mood, and one disconnected line followed another into his mind, giving him a vague sense of melancholy pleasure. He said one or two of them aloud, calling the attention of his nurses—but it was not to them he was speaking. Finally, his mind centred on one which first of all seemed to strike him for its melody alone:—

For who, to dumb forgetfulness a prey,
This pleasing, anxious being e'er resigned,
Left the warm precincts of the cheerful day,
Nor cast one longing, lingering look behind?

He said this aloud once or twice over. "'To dumb forgetfulness a prey!' that is not my feeling—not my feeling; the rest is very true. Gray does not get half justice nowadays. How it satisfies the ear, flowing round and soft! 'To dumb forgetfulness!' now I wonder what he meant by that?"

"You are better, papa," said Rose, softly. Her mother stayed behind, not able to speak; but the girl, in her simplicity, thought the poetry "a good sign."

"No, Rose. 'Dumb forgetfulness,'—it is not that, child; that is not what one fears; to be sure there is a coldness and blackness that might chime in with the words. But the rest is true, 'the warm precincts of the cheerful day;' warm is a living word altogether; it is not warm out here."

"I will put the quilt on the bed," said wistful Rose, thinking he complained of cold.

"No," he said, roused, with a gentle laugh; "the quilt will do nothing for me; I am not cold—not yet; I suppose I shall be presently. Is your mother there? My dear, help me with your experience. I dislike cold so much; does one feel it creeping up before one dies?"

"Oh, Herbert, dearest!" said his wife, heart-broken. What could she answer to such a question?

"Nay, I don't want to make an unnecessary fuss," he said; "it is only a curiosity I have. Cold creeping up—it is disagreeable to think of it. What! I have I more medicine to take? What does Marsden mean by sending me his detestable compounds still? It will only make your bill the larger, and me the less comfortable. I will not have it; take it away."

"It is something different," said Mrs. Damerel. "The doctor thought perhaps it might be worth trying."

"Is it the elixir of life?" said the patient, smiling; "nothing short of that would be worth trying; even that would be too much trouble for the good. It would be folly to come back now, when one has got over all the worst of the way."

"You do not feel worse, Herbert?"

"Oh, no; when I tell you the worst is over, my anxious Martha! I am curious—curious—nothing more. I wish I could but tell you, after, what sort of a thing it was. Sit down by me, and give me your hand. Rose, you will be good; you will do everything your mother says?"

"Oh, Herbert!" said his wife, "do not think of us—if it has come to this—think of yourself, think where you are going—to God, Herbert, dearest, to be happy beyond anything we can think."

"Is it so?" he said, still smiling. "I don't know where I am going, my dear, and that is the only thing that gives me a little trouble. I should like to know. I am not afraid of God, who has always been far better to me than I deserved; and I hope I know the way of life." This he said with a momentary seriousness which was quite exceptional. Then he added, in the musing tone which to his anxious watchers seemed almost a gentle delirium, "But think, my dear! to be sent even into a new place, a strange town, in the dark, without any direction—without knowing where to go, right hand or left." He gave a little, soft, broken laugh. "It is the strangest way of dealing with curious, inquisitive creatures like men. I never realized it before."

Here some one appeared, beckoning behind the curtains, to say that Mr. Nolan was in the next room. The curate came daily, and was always admitted. Rose went softly out to meet him, and almost dropped into the kind man's arms in her exhaustion and excitement. "He is talking so very strangely," she said, the tears running down her pale cheeks. "Oh, Mr. Nolan, I think he is wandering in his mind! Should I send for the doctor? To hear him speak is enough to break one's heart."

The good curate put her in a chair and soothed her, smoothing her pretty hair, with unconscious tenderness, as if she had been a child.

"Don't cry, dear," he said; "or rather, do cry, poor child, it will do you good; and stay quiet till I come back."

Rose did what she was told with the docility of helplessness. She lay back in the chair, and cried softly. In this new strait she was as a child, and all the child's overwhelming sense of desolation, and half-superstitious awe of the terrible event which was coming, weighed down her heart. Pity, and terror, and grief mingled in her mind, till it seemed unable to contain so much emotion. She sat and listened to the low voices in the next room, and watched the side gleam of light which came from the half-open door. The very world seemed hushed while this drama came to its conclusion, and there was not a sound without or within but the soft movements in the sick-room, and the low voices. How many new experiences had come into her simple life in so short a time! Darkness overshadowed the earth already, so that her pleasant pathway in it seemed lost; and now here was Death, that visitor who is always so doubly appalling the first time he enters a peaceful house.

"Well, Nolan, you have come in time, for I am just setting out," said the rector, in a voice stronger than it had been, his anxious wife thought.

"Why, man, don't look so grave; and you, my dear, don't cry, to discourage me. Set me out on my journey a little more cheerily! I never thought much about dying people before; and mind what I say, Nolan, because it is your work. Of course, to those who have never thought about such matters before, religion is all-important; but there's more in it than that. When a man's dying he wants humoring. Such strange fancies come into one's head. I am not at all troubled or serious to speak of; but it is a very odd thing, if you think of it, to set out on such a journey without the least notion where you are to go!"

And he laughed again. It was not harsh nor profane, but a soft laugh, as easy as a child's. I do not know why it should have horrified the attendants so, or what there is wrong in a laugh so gentle from a death-bed; but the hearers both shivered with natural pain and almost terror. They tried to lead him to more serious thoughts, but in vain. His mind, which had been serious enough before, had got somehow dissipated, intoxicated by the approach of the unknown. He could think of nothing else. A certain levity even mingled in his excitement. He asked questions almost with eagerness—questions no one could answer—about the accessories of death. He was curious beyond description about all that he would have to go through. "What a pity that I shall never be able to tell you what it is, and how I liked it!" he said, reflectively; "at least until you know all about it, too; we can compare notes then." He would not give up this kind of talk. After the prayers for the sick, which Mr. Nolan read, he resumed the same subject; and if it is possible to imagine anything that could have made this terrible moment of her life more bitter to poor Mrs. Damerel, I think this would have been the one thing.

"Are his affairs in order, do you know?" said the doctor, after paying his late visit, as the curate accompanied him to the door. He had just given it as his opinion that his patient could not see another morning; and Mr. Nolan had made up his mind to remain at the rectory all night.

"I shouldn't think it; he has never taken much trouble with his affairs."

"Then don't you think you could speak to him even now? I never saw a man so clear-headed, and in such possession of his faculties, so near—

Speak to him, Nolan. He knows exactly how things are, and no agitation can harm him now. He must have some wishes about his family—some arrangements to make."

Mr. Nolan restrained with difficulty an exclamation that rose to his lips, and which might have sounded unkind to a dying man; and then he asked abruptly, "Do you find, in your experience, that people who are dying are much concerned about those they leave behind?"

"Well, no," said the doctor, doubtfully; "I don't think they are. Self gets the upper hand. It is all Nature can do at that moment to think how she is to get through"—

"I suppose so," said the curate, with that seriousness which naturally accompanies such a speculation. He walked with the doctor to the gate, and came back across the plot of shrubbery, musing, with a heavy heart, on the living and on the dying. It was a lovely starlight night, soft and shadowy, but with a brisk little questioning air which kept the leaves a-rustle. Mr. Nolan shivered with something like cold, as he looked up at the stars. "I wonder, after all, where he is going?" he said to himself, with a sympathetic ache of human curiosity in his heart.

CHAPTER VIII.

MR. DAMEREL did not die for twenty-four hours after this. People do not get out of the world so easy. He was not to escape the mortal restlessness, "the fog in his throat," any more than others; and the hours were slow and long, and lingered like years. But at last the rector came to an end of his wondering, and knew, like all the *illuminati* before him who have learned too, but are hushed and make no sign. It is a strange thought for mortals to take in, that almost every death is, for the moment at least, a relief to those who surround the dying. The most intolerable moment is that which precedes the end, and most of as are thankful when it is over. I need not enter into the dismal hush that fell upon the pleasant rectory, nor say how the curious sun besieged the closed windows to get into the house once so freely open to the light; nor how, notwithstanding the long interval of illness which had banished him from common view, the shady corner under the lime-trees, where Mr. Damerel's chair and round table still stood, wore a look of piteous desolation, as if he had left them but yesterday. All this is easily comprehensible. The servants cried a little, and were consoled by their new mourning; the children wept bitterly, then began to smile again; and two poor clergymen, with large families, grew sick with anxiety as to who should have Dinglefield, before our rector had been dead a day (neither of them had it, you may be sure, they wanted it so much). When the news was known in the parish, and especially on the Green, there was a moment of awe and emotion very real in its way. Most people heard of it when they were first called, and thought of it with varying degrees of impression till breakfast, to which they all came down looking very serious, and told each other the details, and remarked to each other what an inscrutable thing it was, and yet that it was wonderful he had lasted so long. Breakfast broke in upon this universal seriousness; for when it is not any connection, as Mrs. Perronet well remarked, you cannot be expected to remain under the impression like those who are relatives; and after breakfast the Green with one consent turned from the dead to the living, and began to ask what Mrs. Damerel would do, how she would be "left," what change it would make to her circumstances? Many shook their heads and feared that it would make a very great change. They calculated what he had had, and what she had had, when they were married, which was an event within the recollection of many; and what the income of the rectory was, after deducting the curate's salary and other necessary expenses; and how much Bertie cost at Eaton; and many other questions which only an intimate knowledge of their neighbors' affairs could have warranted them in discussing. General Perronet knew for certain that Mr. Damerel's life was insured in at least two offices; and though they could not, everybody agreed, have saved anything, yet there arose after a while a general hope that the family would not be so very badly off. Some of the ladies had quite decided before luncheon that the best thing Mrs. Damerel could do would be to take the White House, which happened to be empty, and which contained a number of little rooms just suitable for a large family. To be sure, it was possible that she might prefer to go back to her own county, where her brothers still lived, one of whom was a squire of small property, and the other the parson of the hereditary parish; but the Dinglefield people scarcely thought she would take this step, considering how many friends she had on the Green, and how much better it was to stay where you are known, than to go back to a place where people have forgotten you.

"And then there is Mr. Incledon," said Mrs. Wodehouse, who felt that her son had been slighted, and may be excused perhaps for being a little spiteful. "The mother has always had her eye upon him since he came back to Whitton. You will see that will be a match, if she can manage it; and of course it would be a great match for Miss Rose."

I think if an angel from heaven came down into a country parish and a good woman with daughters entertained him unawares, her neighbors would decide at once which of the girls she meant to marry Gabriel to. But Mrs. Wodehouse had more justification than most gossips have. She could not forget the little pleading note which her Edward had made her write, entreating Rose to come down if only for one moment, and that the girl had taken no notice of it; though before that expedition to Whitton to see the Perugino and Mr. Incledon's great house, Rose had been very well satisfied to have the young sailor at her feet. Mrs. Wodehouse had met the mother and daughter but seldom since, for they had been absorbed in attendance upon the rector; but when by chance she did encounter them, she felt proud to think that she had never said anything but "Good morning." No inquiries after their health had come from her lips. She had retired into polite indifference; though sometimes her heart had been touched by poor Rose's pale cheek, and her wistful look, which seemed to ask pardon. "I do not mind what is done to me," Mrs. Wodehouse said to her dear friend and confidant, Mrs. Musgrove; "but those who slight my son I will never forgive. I do not see that it is unchristian. It is unchristian not to forgive what is done to yourself; and I am sure no one is less ready to take personal offence than I am." She was resolved, therefore, that whatever happened, "Good morning" was all the greeting she would give to the Damerels; though of course she was very sorry indeed for them, and as anxious as other people as to how they would be left, and where they would go.

Mrs. Damerel herself was overwhelmed by her grief in a way which could scarcely have been expected from a woman who had so many other considerations to rouse her out of its indulgence, and who had not been for a long time a very happy wife. But when man and wife have been partially separated as these two had been, and have ceased to feel the sympathy for each other which such a close relationship requires, a long illness has a wonderful effect often in bringing back to the survivor the early image of the being he or she has loved. Perhaps I ought to say she; I do not know if a sick wife is so touching to a husband's imagination as a sick man is to his wife's. And then a little thing had occurred before the end which had gone to Mrs. Damerel's heart more than matters of much greater moment. Her husband had called Rose, and on Rose going to him had waved her away, saying, "No, no," and holding out his feeble hands to her mother. This insignificant little incident had stolen away everything but tenderness from the woman's mind, and she wept for her husband as she might have wept for him had he died in the earlier years of their marriage, with an absorbing grief that drove everything else out of her thoughts. This, however, could not last. When the blinds were drawn up from the rectory, and the brisk sunshine shone in again, and the family looked with unveiled faces upon the lawn, where every one still expected to see him, so full was it of his memory, the common cares of life came back, and had to be thought of. Mrs. Damerel's brothers had both come to the funeral. One of them, the squire, was the trustee under her marriage settlement, and one of the executors of Mr. Damerel's will; so he remained along with the lawyer and the doctor and Mr. Nolan, and listened to all the provisions of that will, which were extremely reasonable, but of a far back date, and which the lawyer read with an occasional shake of his head, which at the moment no one could understand. Unfortunately, however, it was but too easy to understand. The rector, with the wisest care, had appropriated the money he had to the various members of his family. The life interest of the greater part was to be the mother's; a small portion was to be given to the girls on their marriage, and to the boys on their outset in life, and the capital to be divided among them at Mrs. Damerel's death. Nothing could be more sensible or properly arranged. Mr. Hunsdon, Mrs. Damerel's brother, cleared his ruffled brow as he heard it. He had been possessed by an alarmed sense of danger—a feeling that his sister and her family were likely to come upon him—which weighed very heavily upon the good man's mind; but now his brow cleared. Further revelations, however, took away this serenity. The money which Mr. Damerel had divided so judiciously was almost all spent, either in unsuccessful speculations, of which he had made several with a view to increase dividends; or by repeated encroachments on the capital made to pay debts; or for one plausible reason after another. Of the insurances on his life only one had been kept up, and that chiefly because his bankers held it as security for some advance, and had consequently seen that the premium was regularly paid. These discoveries fell like so many thunderbolts upon the little party. I don't think Mrs. Damerel was surprised. She sat with her eyes cast down and her hands clasped, with a flush of shame and trouble on her face.

"Did you know of this, Rose?" her brother asked, sternly, anxious to find some one to blame.

"I feared it," she said, slowly, not lifting her eyes. The flush on her cheek dried up all her tears.

Mr. Hunsdon, for one, believed that she was ashamed—not for the dead man's sake—but because she had shared in the doing of it, and was confounded to find her ill doings brought into the light of day.

"But, good heavens!" he said in her ear, "did you know you were defrauding your children when you wasted your substance like this? I could not have believed it. Was my brother-in-law aware of the state of the affairs? and what did he intend his family to do?"

"Mr. Damerel was not a business man," said the lawyer. "He ought to have left the management in our hands. That mining investment was a thing we never would have recommended, and the neglect of the insurance is most unfortunate. Mr. Damerel was never a man of business."

In the presence of his wife it was difficult to say more.

"A man may not be a man of business, and yet not be a fool," said Squire Hunsdon, hastily. "I beg your pardon, Rose; I don't want to be unkind."

"Let me go, before you use such language," she said, rising hastily. "I cannot bear it. Whatever he has done that is amiss, he is not standing here to answer before us now."

"I mean no offence, Rose. Nay, sit down; don't go away. You can't imagine—a man I had so much respect for—that I mean to cast any reflections. We'll enter into that afterwards," said Mr. Hunsdon. "Let us know at least what they will have to depend on, or if anything is left."

"There is very little left," said Mrs. Damerel, facing the men, who gazed at her wondering, with her pale face and widow's cap. "We had not very much at first, and it is gone; and you must blame me, if any one is to blame. I was not, perhaps, a good manager. I was careless. I did not calculate as I ought to have done. But if the blame is mine, the punishment will also be mine. Do not say anything more about it, for no one here will suffer but my children and me."

"I don't know about that. You must be patient, and you must not be unreasonable," said her brother. "Of course we cannot see you want; though neither George nor I have much to spare; and it is our duty to inquire."

"Will inquiring bring back the money that is lost?" she said. "No, no; you shall not suffer by me. However little it is, we will manage to live on it; we will never be a burden upon any one. I don't think I can bear any more."

And the judges before whom she stood (and not only she, but one who could not answer for himself) were very compassionate to the widow, though Mr. Hunsdon was still curious and much disturbed in his mind. They slurred over the rest, and allowed Mrs. Damerel and her son and daughter to go, and broke up the gloomy little assembly. Mr. Hunsdon took Mr. Nolan by the arm and went out with him, leading him on to the lawn, without any thought how the sound of his steps would echo upon the hearts of the mourners. He would have seated himself in the chair which still stood under the lime-trees had not Mr. Nolan managed to sway his steps away from it, and lead him down the slope to the little platform round the old thorn-tree which was invisible from the windows. The good curate was deeply moved for both the living and the dead.

"I don't mind speaking to you," said the anxious brother; "I have heard so much of you as an attached friend. You must have known them thoroughly, and their way of living. I can't think it was my sister's fault."

"And I know," said Mr. Nolan, with energy, "it was not her fault. It was not any one's fault. He had a generous, liberal way with him"—

"Had he?" said the squire, doubtfully. "He had a costly, expensive way with him; is that what you mean? I am not saying anything against my late brother-in-law. We got on very well, for we saw very little of each other. He had a fine mind, and that sort of thing. I suppose they have kept an extravagant house."

"No, I assure you"—

"Entertained a good deal. Kept a good table, I am certain; good wine—I never drank better claret than that we had last night—the sort of wine *I* should keep for company, and bring up only on grand occasions. If there is much of it remaining I don't mind buying a few dozen at their own price," Mr. Hunsdon said, parenthetically. "I see; fine cookery, good wine, all the luxuries of the season, and the place kept up like a duke's—an expensive house."

"No," said the curate, reiterating an obstinate negative; and then he said, hotly, "she did herself a great deal of injustice. She is the best of managers—the most careful—making everything go twice as far and look twice as well as anybody else."

Mr. Hunsdon looked at him curiously, for he was one of those people who think a man must be "in love with" any woman whose partisan he makes himself. He made a private note of the curate's enthusiasm, and concluded it was best that his sister and her daughter should be warned of his sentiments. "I have not seen very much of my poor brother-in-law for some time," he said, disguising his scrutiny, "so that I have no way of judging for myself. I don't know which is most to blame. In such cases the wife can generally stop the extravagance if she likes. Two boys at Eton, for example—*I* can't afford so much."

"Bertie is on the foundation, and costs very little. He is a boy who will do something in the world yet; and I ought to know, for I taught him his first Greek. As for Reginald, his godfather pays his expenses, as I suppose you know."

"You have been here for a long time, I perceive," said the squire, "if you taught the boy his first Greek, as you say?"

"Eight years," said Mr. Nolan, with a shrug of his shoulders.

"And now?"

"Now? I'll go off again, I suppose, like a rollin' stone, unless the new rector will have me. God help us, what heartless brutes we are!" said the curate, with fiery heat; "I've just laid my old rector in the grave, and I think of the new one before the day's gone. God forgive me; it's the way of the world."

"And why shouldn't you be rector yourself? No one would be so good for the parish, I am sure."

"Me!" said Mr. Nolan, his face lighting up with a broad gleam of humor, which he quenched next moment in the half-conventional gravity which he felt to be befitting to the occasion. "The days of miracles are over, and I don't expect to be made an exception. No; I'll get a district church maybe sometime, with plenty of hard work and little pay; but I am not the kind that are made to be rectors. There is no chance for me."

"The people would like it," said Mr. Hunsdon, who was fishing for information; "it would be a popular appointment, and my sister and I would do anything that might lie in our power."

Mr. Nolan shook his head. "Not they," he said. "They have a kindness for me in my humble condition. They know I'm a friend when they want one; but they want something more to look at for their rector—and so do I too."

"You are not ambitious?" said Mr. Hunsdon, perplexed by his new acquaintance, who shrugged his shoulders again, and rose hastily from the seat under the thorn-tree where they had been sitting.

"That depends," he said, with impatient vagueness; "but I have my work waiting if I can be of no more use here. For whatever I can do, Mrs. Damerel knows I am at her orders. And you won't let her be worried just yet a while?" he added, with a pleading tone, to which his mellow brogue lent an insinuating force which few people could resist. "You'll not go till it's fixed what they are to do?"

"You may be sure I shall do my duty by my sister," said the squire, who, though he had been willing to take the curate's evidence about the most intimate details of his sister's life, instantly resented Mr. Nolan's "interference" when it came on his side. "He is in love with one or the other, or perhaps with both," said the man of the world to himself; "I must put Rose on her guard;" which accordingly he tried to do, but quite ineffectually, Mrs. Damerel's mind being totally unable to take in the insinuation which he scarcely ventured to put in plain words. But, with the exception of this foolish mistake and of a great deal of implied blame which it was not in the nature of the man to keep to himself, he did try to do his duty as became a man with a certain amount of ordinary affection for his sister, and a strong sense of what society required from him as head of his family. However he might disapprove of her, and the extravagance in which she had undeniably been act and part, yet he could not abandon so near a relation. I should not like to decide whether benefits conferred thus from a strong sense of duty have more or less merit than those which flow from an affectionate heart and generous nature, but certainly they have less reward of gratitude. The Green was very much impressed by Mr. Hunsdon's goodness to his sister, but I fear that to her his goodness was a burden more painful than her poverty. And yet he was very good. He undertook, in his brother's name and his own, to pay Bertie's expenses at Eton, where the boy was doing so well; and when it was decided, as the Green by infallible instinct had felt it must be, that the White House was the natural refuge for Mrs. Damerel when the time came to leave the rectory, Mr. Hunsdon made himself responsible for the rent, and put it in order for her with true liberality. The whole parish admired and praised him for this, and said how fortunate Mrs. Damerel was to have so good a brother. And she tried herself to feel it, and to be grateful as he deserved. But gratitude, which springs spontaneous for the simplest of gifts, and exults over a nothing, is often very slow to follow great benefits. Poor Mrs. Damerel thought it was the deadness of her grief which made her so insensible to her brother's kindness. She thought she had grown incapable of feeling; and she had so much to realize, so much to accustom herself to. A change so great and fundamental confuses the mind. So far as she could see before her, she had nothing now to look forward to in life but an endless, humiliating struggle; and she forgot, in the softening of her heart, that for years past she had been struggling scarcely less hardly. When she looked back she seemed to see only happiness in comparison with this dull deprivation of all light and hope in which she was left now. But the reader knows that she had not been happy, and that this was but, as it were, a prismatic reflection from her tears, a fiction of imagination and sorrow; and by and by she began to see more clearly the true state of affairs.

They stayed at the rectory till Christmas by grace of the new rector, who unfortunately, however, could not keep on Mr. Nolan, of whose preferment there never had been a glimmer of hope, beyond that period. Christmas is a dreary time to go into a new home; though I don't think the rector of Dinglefield thought so, who brought home his bride to the pretty rectory, and thought no life could begin more pleasantly than by those cheerful Christmas services in the church, which was all embowered in holly and laurel, in honor of the great English festival and in honor of him; for the Green had of course taken special pains with the decorations on account of the new-comer. The long and dreary autumn which lay between their bereavement and their removal was, however, very heavy and terrible for the Damerels. Its rains and fogs and dreary days seemed to echo and increase their own heaviness of heart; and autumn as it sinks into winter is all the more depressing in a leafy woodland country, as it has been beautiful in its earlier stages. Even the little children were subdued, they knew not why, and felt the change in die house, though it procured them many privileges, and they might now even play in the drawing-room unreproved, and were never sent away hurriedly lest they should disturb papa, as had been the case of old when sometimes they would snatch a fearful joy by a romp in the twilight corners; even the babies felt that this new privilege was somehow a symptom of some falling off and diminution in the family life. But no one felt it as Rose did, who had been shaken out of all the habits of her existence, without having as yet found anything to take their place. She had not even entered upon the idea of duty when her secret romance was brought to a sudden close, and that charmed region of imagination in which youth so readily finds a refuge, and which gilds the homeliest present with dreams of that which may be hereafter, had been arbitrarily closed to the girl. Had her little romance been permitted to her, she would have had a secret spring of hope and content to fall back upon, and would have faced her new life bravely, with a sense of her own individuality, such as seemed now to have faded altogether out of her mind. Her very appearance changed, as was inevitable. Instead of the blooming maiden we have known, it was the whitest of Roses that went about the melancholy house in her black dress, with all the color and life gone out of her, doing whatever she was told with a docility which was sad to see. When she was left to herself she would sit idle or drop absorbed into a book; but everything that was suggested to her she did, without hesitation and without energy. The whole world had become confined to her within these oppressive walls, within this sorrowful house. The people on the Green looked at her with a kind of wondering reverence, saying how she must have loved her father, and how she looked as if she would never get over it. But grief was not all of the weight which crushed her. She was for the moment bound as by some frost, paralyzed in all the springs of her interrupted being. She had no natural force of activity in her to neutralize the chill her soul had taken. She did all that she was told to do, and took every suggestion gratefully; but she had not yet learned to see for herself with her own eyes what had to be done, nor did she realize all the changes that were involved in the one great change which had come upon them. Misfortune had fallen upon her while she was still in the dreamy vagueness of her youth, when the within is more important than the without, and the real and imaginary are so intermingled that it is hard to tell where one ends and another begins. Necessity laid no wholesome, vigor-giving hand upon her, because she was preoccupied with fancies which seemed more important than the reality. Agatha, all alert and alive in her practical matter-of-fact girlhood, was of more value in the house than poor Rose, who was like a creature in a dream, not seeing anything till it was pointed out to her; obeying always and humbly, but never doing or originating anything from her own mind. Nobody understood her, not even herself; and sometimes she would sit down and cry for her father, thinking he would have known what it meant, without any recollection of the share her father had in thus paralyzing her young life. This strange condition of affairs was unknown, however, to any one out-of-doors except Mr. Nolan, who, good fellow, took it upon him once to say a few coaxing, admonishing words to her.

"You'll ease the mother when you can, Miss Rose, dear," he said, taking her soft, passive hands between his own. "You don't mind me saying so—an old fellow and an old friend like me, that loves every one of you, one better than another? I'll hang on if I can, if the new man will have me, and be of use—what's the good of me else?—and you'll put your shoulder to the wheel with a good heart, like the darling girl that you are?"

"My shoulder to the wheel," said Rose, with a half-smile, "and with a good heart! when I feel as if I had no heart at all?" and the girl began to cry, as she did now for any reason, if she was startled, or any one spoke to her suddenly. What could poor Mr. Nolan do but soothe and comfort her? Poor child! they had taken away all the inner strength from her before the time of trial came, and no better influence had yet roused her from the shock, or made her feel that she had something in her which was not to be crushed by any storm. Mr. Nolan knew as little what to make of her as her mother did, who was slowly coming to her old use and wont, and beginning to feel the sharpness of hardship, and to realize once more how it was and why it was that this hardship came.

CHAPTER IX.

The White House did not stand on the Green, but on one of the roads leading out of it, at a short distance from that centre of the world. It looked large from outside—something between a mansion and a cottage—and within was full of useless passages, confused little rooms, and bits of staircases on which the unaccustomed passenger might break his neck with ease, and a general waste of space and disorder of arrangement which pleased the antiquary as quaint, but was much less desirable practically than artistically. There were two sitting-rooms, which were large and low, with raftered roofs, and small, deep-set windows overgrown with creepers; and there was a garden, almost as rambling as the house itself, and surrounded by old walls and hedges which effectually shut out every view, except into its own grassy, mossy depths. Some former enterprising inhabitant had introduced into the drawing-room one long French window, by which there was a practicable exit into the garden; and this was the only modern point in the house. Some people said it spoilt the room, which otherwise would have been perfect; but it was a great convenience and comfort to the Damerels in summer, at least. The house was somewhat damp, somewhat weedy, rather dark; but it was roomy, and more like a house in which gentlefolks could melt away into penury than a pert little new brick house in a street. It was very cheap; for it had various disadvantages, into which I am not called upon to enter. Mrs. Damerel, whose house had always been the perfection of houses, with every new sanitary invention, was glad to put up with these drawbacks for the sake of the low rent—so vast and so many are the changes which absence of money makes. Before Christmas Day they had all the old furniture—save some special pieces of *virtu*, graceful old cabinets, mirrors, and ornamental things, which were sold—arranged and adapted, and settled down in tolerable comfort. The boys, when they came from school, looked with doubtful faces at the change, especially Reginald, who was humiliated by it, and found fault with the room allotted to him, and with the deficiencies of service. "Poor! why are we poor? It must be some one's fault," said this boy to his sister Agatha, who cried, and declared passionately that she wished he had not come back, but had gone to his fine godfather, whom he was always talking of. When an invitation arrived for him from his godfather, some days later, I think they were all glad; for Reginald was very like his father, and could not bear anything mean or poor. The number of servants had dwindled to one, who made believe to be of all work, and did a little of everything. Except in the case of those lucky families who abound in fiction, and now and then, *par exception*, are to be found in ordinary life, who possess a faithful and devoted and all-accomplished woman, who, for love of them, forsakes all hopes of bettering herself, and applies at once genius and knowledge to the multifarious duties of maid-of-all-work— this class of functionary is as great a trouble to her employers as to herself; and to fall back upon attendance so uninstructed and indifferent is one of the hardest consequences of social downfall. The girls had to make up Mary Jane's deficiencies in the White House; and at first, as they were not used to it, the results were but little consolatory. Even Bertie, perhaps, though a good son and a good boy, was not sorry to get back to school, and to the society of his friends, after these first holidays, which had not been happy ones. Poor children! none of them had ever known before what it was to do without what they wanted, and to be content with the bare necessaries of life.

All the same, a shower of cards from all the best people about came pouring down upon the new dwellers in the White House, and were taken in by Mary Jane between a grimy finger and thumb to the drawing-room, where the rumble of the departing carriages excited Agatha and Patty, at least, if no one else. And all the people on the Green made haste to call to express their sympathy and friendliness. Mrs. Wodehouse was the only one who did not ask to see Mrs. Damerel; but even she did not lose a day in calling; and, indeed, it was while on her way from the White House that for the first time she met Rose, who had been out about some business for her mother, and who, with her black veil over her face, was straying slowly home. Mrs. Wodehouse said "Good morning," with a determination to hold by her formula and not be tempted into kindness; but when the girl put back her veil and showed her pale face, the good woman's heart melted in spite of herself.

"How pale you are!" she said. "Oh, Rose! and how is your mother?" she added hastily, trying to save herself from the overflowing of tenderness which came upon her unawares.

"Are you going to see her?" said Rose.

"I have been to call; I did not, of course, expect she would see me. And how do you like the White House? I hope you have not been ill; you do not look so fresh as when I saw you last."

"It is very nice," said Rose, answering the first question; "though it feels damp just at first; we all think we shall soon get used to it. It is a long time since I saw you last."

This was said with a little piteous smile which made Mrs. Wodehouse's resolution "never to forgive" become more and more hard to keep.

"I could not think I was wanted," she said with an effort to appear short and stern, "or I should have gone to your mother before now."

"Why?" asked Rose, with a wondering glance; and then, as there was a dead pause, which was awkward, she said, softly: "I hope you have news from—your son?"

"Oh, yes; I have news from him. He is always very good in writing. There never was a kinder boy to his mother. He never forgets me; though there are many people who would fain get his attention. Edward is always finding friends wherever he goes."

"I am glad," said poor Rose.

"Plenty of friends! I have nothing but good news of him. He writes in the best of spirits. Oh, Rose!" cried Mrs. Wodehouse, hurriedly running one subject into another with breathless precipitancy, "how could you be so heartless—so unkind—as not to come down-stairs when I asked you to bid my poor boy good-by?"

A flush of color came upon Rose's pale face; it made her look like herself again. "I could not," she said; "do not be angry. I have so wanted to tell you. There was nobody there but me, and he held my hand, and would not let me leave him. I could not. Oh! how glad I am that you have asked me! It was not my fault." Her father's name brought the big tears to her eyes. "Poor papa!" she added, softly, with an instinctive sense that he needed defence.

Whether Mrs. Wodehouse would have taken her to her arms forthwith on the open Green in the wintry afternoon light, if no one had disturbed them, I cannot tell; but, just as she was putting out her hands to the girl, they were interrupted by a third person, who had been coming along the road unnoticed, and who now came forward, with his hat in his hand, and with the usual inquiry about her mother to which Rose was accustomed. The sound of his voice made Mrs. Wodehouse start with suppressed anger and dismay; and Rose looked out from the heavy shadow of the crape veil, which showed the paleness of her young face, as if under a penthouse or heavy-shaded cavern. But she was not pale at that moment; a light of emotion was in her face. The tears were hanging on her eyelashes; her soft lip was quivering. Mr. Incledon thought that grief and downfall had done all that the severest critic could have desired for her young beauty. It had given tenderness, expression, feeling to the blooming rose face, such as is almost incompatible with the first radiance of youth.

"Would Mrs. Damerel see me, do you think?" he asked; "or is it too early to intrude upon her? It is about business I want to speak."

"I will ask," said Rose. "But if it is about business she will be sure to see you. She says she is always able for that."

"Then I will say good-by," said Mrs. Wodehouse, unreasonably excited and angry, she could scarcely tell why. She made a step forward, and then came back again with a little compunction, to add, in an undertone: "I am glad we have had this little explanation. I will tell him when I write, and it will please him, too."

"You have not been quarrelling with Mrs. Wodehouse, that you should have little explanations?" said Mr. Incledon, as he walked along to the White House by Rose's side.

"Oh, no! it was nothing;" but he saw the old rose flush sweep over the cheeks which had half relapsed into paleness. What was it? and who did

Mrs. Wodehouse mean to write to? and what was she glad about? These foolish questions got into the man's head, though they were too frivolous to be thought of. She took him into the drawing-room at the White House, which was almost dark by this time, it was so low; and where the cheery glimmer of the fire made the room look much more cheerful than it ever was in the short daylight, through the many branches that surrounded the house. Mrs. Damerel was sitting alone there over the fire; and Rose left him with her mother, and went away, bidding Agatha watch over the children that no one might disturb mamma. "She is talking to Mr. Incledon about business," said Rose, passing on to her own room; and Agatha, who was sharp of wit, could not help wondering what pleasant thing had happened to her sister to make her voice so soft and thrilling. "I almost expected to hear her sing," Agatha said afterwards; though indeed a voice breaking forth in a song, as all their voices used to do, six months ago, would have seemed something impious at this moment, in the shadow that lay over the house.

Mr. Incledon was nearly an hour "talking business" with Mrs. Damerel, during which time they sat in the firelight and had no candles, being too much interested in their conversation to note how time passed. Mrs. Damerel said nothing about the business when the children came in to tea —the homely and inexpensive meal which had replaced dinner in the White House. Her eyes showed signs of tears, and she was very quiet, and let the younger ones do and say almost what they pleased. But if the mother was quiescent, Rose, too, had changed in a different way. Instead of sitting passive, as she usually did, it was she who directed Agatha and Patty about their lessons, and helped Dick, and sent the little ones off at their proper hour to bed. There was a little glimmer of light in her eyes, a little dawn of color in her cheek. The reason was nothing that could have been put into words—a something perfectly baseless, visionary, and unreasonable. It was not the hope of being reconciled to Edward Wodehouse, for she had never quarrelled with him; nor the hope of seeing him again, for he was gone for years. It was merely that she had recovered her future, her imagination, her land of promise. The visionary barrier which had shut her out from that country of dreams had been removed—it would be hard to say how; for good Mrs. Wodehouse certainly was not the door-keeper of Rose's imagination, nor had it in her power to shut and open at her pleasure. But what does how and why matter in that visionary region? It was so, which is all that need be said. She was not less sorrowful, but she had recovered herself. She was not less lonely, nor did she feel less the change in her position; but she was once more Rose, an individual creature, feeling the blood run in her veins, and the light lighten upon her, and the world spread open before her.

If I have freedom in my love,
And in my soul am free—

I suppose this was how she felt. She had got back that consciousness which is sometimes bitter and sometimes sad, but without which we cannot live—the consciousness that she was no shadow in the world, but herself; no reflection of another's will and feelings, but possessor of her own.

When her mother and she were left alone, Rose got up from where she was sitting and drew a low chair, which belonged to one of the children, to her mother's knee. Mrs. Damerel, too, had watched Agatha's lingering exit with some signs of impatience, as if she, too, had something to say; but Rose had not noticed this, any more than her mother had noticed the new impulse which was visible in her child. The girl was so full of it that she began to speak instantly, without waiting for any question.

"Mamma," she said, softly, "I have not been a good daughter to you; I have left you to take all the trouble, and I have not tried to be of use. I want to tell you that I have found it out, and that I will try with all my heart to be different from to-day."

"Rose, my dear child!"—Mrs. Damerel was surprised and troubled. The tears, which rose so easily now, came with a sudden rush to her eyes. She put her arms around the girl, and drew her close, and kissed her. "I have never found fault with you, my darling," she said.

"No, mamma; and that makes me feel it more. But it shall be different; I am sorry, more sorry than I can tell you; but it shall be different from to-day."

"But, Rose, what has put this into your head to-day?"

A wavering blush came and went upon Rose's face. She had it almost in her heart to tell her mother; but yet there was nothing to tell, and what could she say?

"I—can't tell, mamma. It is mild and like spring. I think it was being out, and hearing people speak—kindly"—

Here Rose paused, and, in her turn, let fall a few soft tears. She had gone out very little, scarcely stirring beyond the garden, since her father's death, and Mrs. Damerel thought it was the mere impulse of reviving life; unless indeed—

"My dear, did Mr. Incledon say anything to you!" she asked, with a vague hope.

"Mr. Incledon? Oh, no! except to ask me if you would see him—on business. What was his business?" said innocent Rose, looking up into her mother's face.

"Rose," said Mrs. Damerel, "I was just about to speak to you on a very important matter when you began. My dear, I must tell you at once what Mr. Incledon's business was. It was about you."

"About me?" All the color went out of Rose's face in a moment; she recollected the visit to Whitton, and the sudden light that had flashed upon her as he and she looked at the picture together. She had forgotten all about it months ago, and indeed had never again thought of Mr. Incledon. But now in a moment her nerves began to thrill and her heart to beat; yet she herself, in whom the nerves vibrated and the heart throbbed, to turn to stone.

"Rose, you are not nervous or silly like many girls, and you know now what life is—not all a happy dream, as it sometimes seems at the beginning. My dear, I have in my hand a brighter future than you ever could have hoped for, if you will have it. Mr. Incledon has asked my leave to ask you to be his wife. Rose"—

"Me! his wife!" Rose clutched at her mother's hand and repeated these words with a pant of fright; though it seemed to her the moment they were said as if she had all her life known they were coming, and had heard them a hundred times before.

"That is what he wants, Rose. Don't tremble so, nor look at me so wildly. It is a wonderful thing to happen to so young a girl as you. He is very good and very kind, and he would be, oh! of so much help to all your family; and he could give you everything that heart can desire, and restore you to far more than you have lost; and he is very fond of you, and would make you an excellent husband. I promised to speak to you, dear. You must think it over. He does not wish you to give him an answer at once."

"Mamma," said Rose, hoarsely, with a sudden trembling which seemed to reach into her very heart, "is it not better to give an answer at once? Mamma, I am not fond of him. I think it would be best to say so now."

"You are not fond of him? Is that all the consideration you give such a question? You do not intend *that* for an answer, Rose?"

"Oh, mamma, is it not enough? What more answer could I give? I am not fond of him at all. I could not pretend to be. When it is an answer like that, surely it is best to give it now."

"And so," said her mother, "you throw aside one of the best offers that ever a girl received, with less thought on the subject than you would give to a cat or a dog! You decide your whole future without one thought. Rose, is this the helpfulness you have just promised me? Is this the thoughtfulness for yourself and all of us that I have a right to expect?"

Rose did not know what to reply. She looked at her mother with eyes suddenly hollowed out by fear and anxiety and trouble, and watched every movement of her lips and hands with a growing alarm which she could not control.

"You do not speak? Rose, Rose, you must see how wrong you would be to act so hastily. If it were a question of keeping or sending away a servant, nay, even a dog, you would give more thought to it; and this is a man who loves, who would make you happy. Oh, do not shake your head! How can a child of your age know? A man who, I am sure, would make you happy; a man who could give you everything and more than everything, Rose. I cannot let you decide without thought."

"Does one need to think?" said Rose, slowly, after a pause. "I do not care for him, I cannot care for him. You would not have me tell a lie?"

"I would have you deny yourself," cried her mother; "I would have you think of some higher rule than your own pleasure. Is that the best thing in the world, to please yourself? Oh, I could tell you stories of that! Why are we in this poor little house with nothing? why is my poor Bertie dependent upon my brother, and you girls forced to work like maid-servants, and our life all changed? Through self-indulgence, Rose. Oh! God forgive me for saying it, but I must tell the truth. Through choosing the pleasure of the moment rather than the duties that we cannot shake off; through deciding always to do what one liked rather than to do what was right. Here are eight of you children with your lives blighted, all that one might be pleasant and unburdened. I have suffered under it all my life. Not anything wrong, not anything wicked, but only, and always and before everything, what one liked one's self."

Mrs. Damerel spoke with a passion which was very unlike her usual calm. The lines came into her brow which Rose remembered of old, but which the tranquillity of grief had smoothed out. A hot color mounted to her cheeks, making a line beneath her eyes. The girl was struck dumb by this sudden vehemence. Her reason was confused by the mingled truth and sophistry, which she felt without knowing how to disentangle them, and she was shocked and wounded by the implied blame thus cast upon him who had been of late the idol of her thoughts, and whom, if she had once timidly begun to form a judgment on him, she had long ceased to think of as anything but perfect.

"Oh! stop, stop! don't say any more!" she cried, clasping her hands.

"I cannot stop," said Mrs. Damerel; "not now, when I have begun. I never thought to say as much to one of his children, and to no other could I ever speak, Rose. I see the same thing in Reginald, and it makes my heart sick; must I find it in you too? There are people who are so happy as to like what they have to do, what it is their duty to do; and these are the blessed ones. But it is not always, it is not often so in this life. Dear, listen to what I say. Here is a way by which you may make up for much of the harm that has been done; you may help all that belong to you; you may put yourself in a position to be useful to many; you may gain what men only gain by the labor of their lives; and all this by marrying a good man whom you will make happy. Will you throw it away because at the first glance it is not what your fancy chooses? Will you set your own taste against everybody's advantage? Oh, my darling, think, think! Do not let your first motive, in the first great thing you are called upon to do, be mere self!"

Mrs. Damerel stopped short, with a dry glitter in her eyes and a voice which was choked and broken. She was moved to the extent of passion— she who in general was so self-restrained. A combination of many emotions worked within her. To her mind, every good thing for her child was contained in this proposal; and in Rose's opposition to it she saw the rising of the poisonous monster which had embittered her whole life. She did not pause to ask herself what there was in the nature of this sacrifice she demanded, which made it less lawful, less noble, than the other sacrifices which are the Christian's highest ideal of duty. It was enough that by this step, which did not seem to Mrs. Damerel so very hard, Rose would do everything for herself and much for her family, and that she hesitated, declined to take it, because it was not pleasant, because she did not like it. Like it! The words raised a perfect storm in the breast of the woman who had been made wretched all her life by her ineffectual struggle against the habitual decision of her husband for what he liked. She was too much excited to hear what Rose had to say; if, indeed, poor Rose had anything to say after this sudden storm which had broken upon her.

"We will speak of it to-morrow, when you have had time to think," she said, kissing her daughter, and dismissing her hastily. When Rose had gone, she fell back into her chair by the waning firelight, and thought over the many times in her own life when she had battled and had been worsted on this eternal point of difference between the two classes of humanity. She had struggled for self-denial against self-indulgence in a hundred different ways on a hundred fields of battle, and here was the end of it: a poor old house, tumbling to pieces about her ears, a poor little pittance, just enough to give her children bread; and for those children no prospect but toil for which they had not been trained, and which changed their whole conception of life. Bertie, her bright boy, for whom everything had been hoped, if her brother's precarious bounty should fail, what was there before him but a poor little clerkship in some office from which he never could rise, and which, indeed, his uncle had suggested at first as a way of making him helpful to his family. God help her! This was what a virtuous and natural preference for the things one liked had brought Mrs. Damerel to; and if her mind took a confused and over-strained view of the subject, and of the lengths to which self-denial ought to be carried, was it any wonder? I think there is a great deal to be said on her side of the case.

Rose, for her part, lit her candle and went up the old stairs—which creaked under her light foot—with her head bent down, and her heart stifled under a weight that was too much for her. A cold, cold January night, the chill air coming in at the old casements, the dark skies without lending no cheering influence, and no warmth of cheery fires within to neutralize Nature's heaviness; an accusation thrown upon her under which her whole being ached and revolted; a duty set before her which was terrible to think of; and no one to advise, or comfort, or help. What was she to do?

CHAPTER X.

MR. INCLEDON was a man of whom people said that any girl might be glad to marry him; and considering marriage from an abstract point of view, as one naturally does when it does not concern one's self, this was entirely true. In position, in character, in appearance, and in principles, he was everything that could be desired: a good man, just, and never consciously unkind; nay, capable of generosity when it was worth his while and he had sufficient inducement to be generous. A man well educated, who had been much about the world, and had learned the toleration which comes by experience; whose opinions were worth hearing on almost every subject; who had read a great deal, and thought a little, and was as much superior to the ordinary young man of society in mind and judgment as he was in wealth. That this kind of man often fails to captivate a foolish girl, when her partner in a valse, brainless, beardless, and penniless, succeeds without any trouble in doing so, is one of those mysteries of nature which nobody can penetrate, but which happens too often to be doubted. Even in this particular, however, Mr. Incledon had his advantages. He was not one of those who, either by contempt for the occupations of youth or by the gravity natural to maturer years, allow themselves to be pushed aside from the lighter part of life—he still danced, though not with the absolute devotion of twenty, and retained his place on the side of youth, not permitting himself to be shelved. More than once, indeed, the young officers from the garrison near, and the young scions of the county families, had looked on with puzzled non-comprehension, when they found themselves altogether distanced in effect and popularity by a mature personage whom they would gladly have called an old fogy had they dared. These young gentlemen of course consoled their vanity by railing against the mercenary character of women who preferred wealth to everything. But it was not only his wealth upon which Mr. Incledon stood. No girl who had married him need have felt herself withdrawn to the grave circle in which her elders had their place. He was able to hold his own in every pursuit with men ten years his juniors, and did so. Then, too, he had almost a romantic side to his character; for a man so well off does not put off marrying for so long without a reason, and though nobody knew of any previous story, any "entanglement," which would have restrained him, various picturesque suggestions were afloat; and even failing these, the object of his choice might have laid the flattering unction to her soul that his long waiting had been for the realization of some perfect ideal, which he found only in her.

This model of a marriageable man took his way from the White House in a state of mind less easily described than most of his mental processes.

He was not excited to speak of, for an interview between a lover of thirty-five and the mother of the lady is not generally exciting; but he was a little doubtful of his own perfect judiciousness in the step he had just taken. I can no more tell you why he had set his heart on Rose than I can say why she felt no answering inclination towards him—for there were many other girls in the neighborhood who would in many ways have been more suitable to a man of his tastes and position. But Rose was the one woman in the world for him, by sheer caprice of nature; just as reasonable, and no more so, as that other caprice which made him, with all his advantages and recommendations, not the man for her. If ever a man was in a position to make a deliberate choice, such as men are commonly supposed to make in matrimony, Mr. Incledon was the man; yet he chose just as much and as little as the rest of us do. He saw Rose, and some power which he knew nothing of decided the question at once for him. He had not been thinking of marriage, but then he made up his mind to marry; and whereas he had on various occasions weighed the qualities and the charms of this one and the other, he never asked himself a question about her, nor compared her with any other woman, nor considered whether she was suited for him, or anything else about her. This was how he exercised that inestimable privilege of choice which women sometimes envy. But, having once received this conviction into his mind, he had never wavered in his determination to win her. The question in his mind now was, not whether his selection was the best he could have made, but whether it was wise of him to have entrusted his cause to the mother rather than to have spoken to Rose herself. He had remained in the background during those dreary months of sorrow. He had sent flowers and game and messages of inquiry; but he had not thrust himself upon the notice of the women, till their change of residence gave token that they must have begun to rouse themselves for fresh encounter with the world. When he was on his way to the White House he had fully persuaded himself that to speak to the mother first was the most delicate and the most wise thing he could do. For one thing, he could say so much more to her than he could to Rose; he could assure her of his good-will and of his desire to be of use to the family, should he become a member of it. Mr. Incledon did not wish to bribe Mrs. Damerel to be on his side. He had indeed a reasonable assurance that no such bribe was necessary, and that a man like himself must always have a reasonable mother on his side. This he was perfectly aware of, as indeed any one in his senses would have been. But as soon as he had made his declaration to Mrs. Damerel, and had left the White House behind, his thoughts began to torment him with doubts of the wisdom of this proceeding. He saw very well that there was no clinging of enthusiastic love, no absolute devotedness of union, between this mother and daughter, and he began to wonder whether he might not have done better had he run all the risks and broached the subject to Rose herself, shy and liable to be startled as she was. It was perhaps possible that his own avowal, which must have had a certain degree of emotion in it, would have found better acceptation with her than the passionless statement of his attentions which Mrs. Damerel would probably make. For it never dawned upon Mr. Incledon's imagination that Mrs. Damerel would support his suit not with calmness, but passionately—more passionately, perhaps, than would have been possible to himself. He could not have divined any reason why she should do so, and naturally he had not the least idea of the tremendous weapons she was about to employ in his favor. I don't think, for very pride and shame, that he would have sanctioned the use of them, had he known.

It happened, however, by chance, that as he walked home in the wintry twilight he met Mrs. Wodehouse and her friend Mrs. Musgrove, who were going the same way as he was, on their way to see the Northcotes, who had lately come to the neighborhood. He could not but join them so far in their walk, nor could he avoid the conversation which was inevitable. Mrs. Wodehouse indeed was very eager for it, and began almost before he could draw breath.

"Did you see Mrs. Damerel after all?" she asked. "You remember I met you when you were on your way?"

"Yes; she was good enough to see me," said Mr. Incledon.

"And how do you think she is looking? I hear such different accounts; some people say very ill, some just as usual. I have not seen her, myself," said Mrs. Wodehouse, slightly drawing herself up, "except in church."

"How was that?" he said, half amused. "I thought you had always been great friends."

Upon this he saw Mrs. Musgrove give a little jerk to her friend's cloak, in warning, and perceived that Mrs. Wodehouse wavered between a desire to tell a grievance and the more prudent habit of self-restraint.

"Oh!" she said, with a little hesitation; "yes, of course we were always good friends. I had a great admiration for our late good rector, Mr. Incledon. What a man he was! Not to say a word against the new one, who is very nice, he will never be equal to Mr. Damerel. What a fine mind he had, and a style, I am told, equal to the very finest preachers! We must never hope to hear such sermons in our little parish again. Mrs. Damerel is a very good woman, and I feel for her deeply; but the attraction in that house, as I am sure you must have felt, was not her, but him."

"I have always had a great regard for Mrs. Damerel," said Mr. Incledon.

"Oh, yes, yes! I am sure—a good wife and an excellent mother and all that; but not the fine mind, not the intellectual conversation, one used to have with the dear rector," said good Mrs. Wodehouse, who had about as much intellect as would lie on a sixpence; and then she added, "perhaps I am prejudiced; I never can get over a slight which I am sure she showed to my son."

"Ah! what was that?"

Mrs. Musgrove once more pulled her friend's cloak, and there was a great deal more eagerness and interest than the occasion deserved in Mr. Incledon's tone.

"Oh, nothing of any consequence! What do you say, dear?—a mistake? Well, I don't think it was a mistake. They thought Edward was going to —yes, *that* was a mistake, if you please. I am sure he had many other things in his mind a great deal more important. But they thought—and though common civility demanded something different, and I took the trouble to write a note and ask it, I do think—but, however, after the words I had with her to-day, I no longer blame Rose. Poor child! I am always very sorry for poor Rose."

"Why should you be sorry for Miss Damerel? Was she one of those who, slighted your son? I hope Mr. Edward Wodehouse is quite well."

"He is very well, I thank you, and getting on so satisfactorily; nothing could be more pleasant. Oh, you must not think Edward cared! He has seen a great deal of the world, and he did not come home to let himself be put down by the family of a country clergyman. That is not at all what I meant; I am sorry for Rose, however, because of a great many things. She ought to go out as a governess or companion, or something of that sort, poor child! Mrs. Damerel may try, but I am sure they never can get on as they are doing. I hear that all they have to depend on is about a hundred and fifty a year. A family can never live upon that, not with their habits, Mr. Incledon; and therefore I think I may well say *poor* Rose!"

"I don't think Miss Damerel will ever require to make such a sacrifice," he said, hurriedly.

"Well, I only hope you are right," said Mrs. Wodehouse. "Of course you know a great deal more about business matters than I do, and perhaps their money is at higher interest than we think for; but if I were Rose I almost think I should see it to be my duty. Here we are at Mrs. Northcote's, dear. Mr. Incledon, I am afraid we must say good-by."

Mr. Incledon went home very hot and fast after this conversation. It warmed him in the misty, cold evening, and seemed to put so many weapons into his hand. Rose, his Rose, go out as a governess or companion! He looked at the shadow of his own great house standing out against the frosty sky, and laughed to himself as he crossed the park. She a dependent, who might to-morrow if she pleased be virtual mistress of Whitton and all its wealth! He would have liked to say to these women, "In three months Rose will be the great lady of the parish, and lay down the law to you and the Green, and all your gossiping society." He would even in a rare fit of generosity have liked to tell them, on the spot, that this blessedness was in Rose's power, to give her honor in their eyes, whether she accepted him or not; which was a very generous impulse indeed, and one which few men would have been equal to—though indeed as a matter of fact Mr. Incledon did not carry it out. But he went into the lonely house where everything pleasant and luxurious, except the one crowning luxury of some one to share it with, awaited him, in a glow of energy and eagerness, resolved to go back again to-morrow and plead his cause with Rose herself, and win her, not prudentially through her mother, but by his own warmth of love and eloquence. Poor Rose in June! In the wintry setting of the White House she was not much like the rector's flower-maiden, in all her delicate perfection of bloom, "queen rose of the rosebud garden," impersonation of all the warmth, and sweetness, and fragrance, and exquisite simple profusion of summer and nature. Mr. Incledon's heart swelled full of love and pity as he thought of the contrast—not with passion, but soft tenderness, and a delicious sense of what it was in his power to do for her, and to restore her to. He strayed over the rooms which he had once shown to her, with a natural pride in their beauty, and in all the delicate treasures he had accumulated there, until he came to the little inner room with its gray-green hangings, in which hung the Perugino, which, since Rose had seen it, he had always called his Raphael. He seemed to see her too, standing there looking at it, a creature partaking something of that soft divinity, an enthusiast with sweet soul and looks congenial to that heavenly art. I do not know that his mind was of a poetical turn by nature, but there are moments when life makes a poet of the dullest; and on this evening the lonely, quiet house within the parks and woods of Whitton, where there had been neither love, nor anything worth calling life, for years, except in the cheery company of the servants' hall, suddenly got itself lighted up with ethereal lights of tender imagination and feeling. The illumination did not show outwardly, or it might have alarmed the Green, which was still unaware that the queen of the house had passed by there, and the place lighted itself up in prospect of her coming.

After dinner, however, Mr. Incledon descended from these regions of fancy and took a step which seemed to himself a very clever as well as prudent, and at the same time a very friendly, one. He had not forgotten, any more than the others had, that summer evening on the lawn at the rectory, when young Wodehouse had strayed down the hill with Rose, out of sight of the seniors of the party, and though all his active apprehensions on that score had been calmed down by Edward's departure, yet he was too wise not to perceive that there was something in Mrs. Wodehouse's disjointed talk more than met the eye at the first glance.

Mr. Incledon had a friend who was one of the Lords of the Admiralty, and upon whom he could rely to do him a service; a friend whom he had never asked for anything—for what was official patronage to the master of Whitton? He wrote him a long and charming letter, which, if I had only room for it, or if it had anything to do except incidentally with this simple history, would give the reader a much better idea of his abilities and social charms than anything I can show of him here. In it he discussed the politics of the moment, and that gossip on a dignified scale about ministers and high officials of state which is half history—and he touched upon social events in a light and amusing strain, with that half cynicism which lends salt to correspondence; and he told his friend half gayly, half seriously, that he was beginning to feel somewhat solitary, and that dreams of marrying, and marrying soon, were stealing into his mind. And he told him about his Perugino ("which I fondly hope may turn out an early Raphael"), and which it would delight him to show to a brother connoisseur. "And, by the bye," he added, after all this, "I have a favor to ask of you which I have kept to the end like a lady's postscript. I want you to extend the ægis of your protection over a fine young fellow in whom I am considerably interested. His name is Wodehouse, and his ship is at present on that detestable slave trade service which costs us so much money and does so little good. He has been a long time in the service, and I hear he is a very promising young officer. I should consider it a personal favor if you could do something for him; and (N. B.) it would be a still greater service to combine promotion with as distant a post as possible. His friends are anxious to keep him out of the way for private reasons—the old 'entanglement' business, which, of course, you will understand; but I think it hard that this sentence of banishment should be conjoined with such a disagreeable service. Give him a gunboat, and send him to look for the Northwest passage, or anywhere else where my lords have a whim for exploring! I never thought to have paid such a tribute to your official dignity as to come, hat in hand, for a place, like the rest of the world. But no man, I suppose, can always resist the common impulse of his kind; and I am happy in the persuasion that to you I will not plead in vain."

I am afraid that nothing could have been more disingenuous than this letter. How it worked, the reader will see hereafter; but, in the mean time, I cannot defend Mr. Incledon. He acted, I suppose, on the old and time-honored sentiment that any stratagem is allowable in love and war, and consoled himself for the possible wrong he might be doing (only a possible wrong, for Wodehouse might be kept for years cruising after slaves, for anything Mr. Incledon knew) by the unquestionable benefit which would accompany it. "A young fellow living by his wits will find a gunboat of infinitely more service to him than a foolish love affair which never could come to anything," his rival said to himself.

And after having sealed this letter, he returned into his fairy land. He left the library where he had written it, and went to the drawing-room which he rarely used, but which was warm with a cheerful fire and lighted with soft wax-lights for his pleasure, should he care to enter. He paused at the door a moment and looked at it. The wonders of upholstery in this carefully decorated room, every scrap of furniture in which had cost its master thought, would afford pages of description to a fashionable American novelist, or to the refined chronicles of the "Family Herald;" but I am not sufficiently learned to do them justice. The master of the house, however, looked at the vacant room with its softly burning lights, its luxurious vacant seats, its closely drawn curtains, the books on the tables which no one ever opened, the pictures on the walls which nobody looked at (except on great occasions), with a curious sense at once of desolation and of happiness. How dismal its silence was! not a sound but the dropping of the ashes from the fire, or the movement of the burning fuel; and he himself a ghost looking into a room which might be inhabited by ghosts for aught he knew. Here and there, indeed, a group of chairs had been arranged by accident so as to look as if they were occupied, as if one unseen being might be whispering to another, noiselessly smiling, and pointing at the solitary. But no, there was a pleasanter interpretation to be given to that soft, luxurious, brightly-colored vacancy; it was all prepared and waiting, ready for the gentle mistress who was to come.

How different from the low-roofed drawing-room at the White House, with the fireplace at one end of the long room, with the damp of ages in the old walls, with draughts from every door and window, and an indifferent lamp giving all the light they could afford! Mr. Incledon, perhaps, thought of that, too, with an increased sense of the advantages he had to offer; but lightly, not knowing all the discomforts of it. He went back to his library after this inspection, and the lights burned on, and the ghosts, if there were any, had the full enjoyment of it till the servants came to extinguish the candles and shut up everything for the night.

CHAPTER XI.

WHEN Rose went up the creaking stairs to bed on that memorable night her feelings were like those of some one who has just been overtaken by one of the great catastrophes of nature—a hurricane or an earthquake—and who, though escaped for the moment, hears the tempest gathering in another quarter, and knows that this is but the first flash of its wrath, and that he has yet worse encounters to meet. I am of Mr. Incledon's opinion—or rather of the doubt fast ripening into an opinion in his mind—that he had made a mistake, and that possibly if he had taken Rose herself "with the tear in her eye," and pressed his suit at first hand, he might have succeeded better; but such might-be's are always doubtful to affirm and impossible to prove. She sat down for a while in her cold room, where the draughts were playing freely about, and where there was no fire—to think; but as for thinking, that was an impossible operation in face of the continued gleams of fancy which kept showing now one scene to her, now another; and of the ringing echo of her mother's words which kept sounding through and through the stillness. Self-indulgence—choosing her own pleasure rather than her duty—what she liked instead of what was right. Rose was far too much confused to make out how it was that these reproaches seemed to her instinct so inappropriate to the question; she only felt it vaguely, and cried a little at the thought of the selfishness attributed to her; for there is no opprobrious word that cuts so deeply into the breast of a romantic, innocent girl. She sat there pensive till all her faculties got absorbed in the dreary sense of cold and bodily discomfort, and then she rose and said her prayers, and untwisted her pretty hair and brushed it out, and went to bed, feeling as if she would have to watch through the long, dark hours till morning, though the darkness and loneliness frightened her, and she dreaded the night. But Rose was asleep in half an hour, though the tears were not dry on her eyelashes, and I think slept all the long night through which she had been afraid of, and woke only when the first gray of daylight revealed the cold room and a cold morning dimly to her sight—slept longer than usual, for emotion tires the young. Poor child! she was a little ashamed of herself when she found how soundly she had slept.

"Mamma would not let me call you," said Agatha, coming into her room; "she said you were very tired last night; but do please come down now, and make haste. There is such a basket of flowers in the hall from Whitton, the man says. Where's Whitton? Isn't it Mr. Incledon's place? But make haste, Rose, for breakfast, now that you are awake."

So she had no time to think just then, but had to hurry down-stairs, where her mother met her with something of a wistful look, and kissed her with a kind of murmured half apology. "I am afraid I frightened you last night, Rose."

"Oh, no, not frightened," the girl said, taking refuge among the children, before whom certainly nothing could be said; and then Agatha and Patty surged into the conversation, and all gravity or deeper meaning was taken out of it. Indeed, her mother was so cheerful that Rose would almost have hoped she was to hear no more of it, had it not been for the cluster of flowers which stood on the table and the heaped-up bunches of beautiful purple grapes which filled a pretty Tuscan basket, and gave dignity to the bread and butter. This was a sign of the times which was very alarming; and I do not know why it was, unless it might be by reason of her youth, that those delicate and lovely things—fit offerings for a lover—never moved her to any thought of what it was she was rejecting, or tempted her to consider Mr. Incledon's proposal as one which involved many delightful things along with himself, who was not delightful. This idea, oddly enough, did not find any place in her mind, though she was as much subject to the influence of all that was lovely and pleasant as any girl could be.

The morning passed, however, without any further words on the subject, and her heart had begun to beat easier and her excitement to calm down, when Mrs. Damerel suddenly came to her, after the children's lessons, which was now their mother's chief occupation. She came upon her quite unexpectedly, when Rose, moved by their noiseless presence in the room, and unable to keep her hands off them any longer, had just commenced, in the course of her other arrangements (for Rose had to be a kind of upper housemaid, and make the drawing-room habitable after the rough and ready operation which Mary Jane called "tidying"), to make a pretty group upon a table in the window of Mr. Incledon's flowers. Certainly they made the place look prettier and pleasanter than it had ever done yet, especially as one stray gleam of sunshine, somewhat pale, like the girl herself, but cheery, had come glancing in to light up the long, low, quaint room and caress the flowers. "Ah, Rose, they have done you good already!" said her mother; "you look more like yourself than I have seen you for many a day."

Rose took her hands from the last flower-pot as if it had burned her, and stood aside, so angry and vexed to have been found at this occupation that she could have cried.

"My dear," said her mother, going up to her, "I do not know that Mr. Incledon will be here to-day; but if he comes I must give him an answer. Have you reflected upon what I said to you? I need not tell you again how important it is, or how much you have in your power."

Rose clasped her hands together in self-support, one hand held fast by the other, as if that slender grasp had been something worth clinging to. "Oh! what can I say?" she cried; "I—told you; what more can I say?"

"You told me! Then, Rose, everything that I said to you last night goes for nothing, though you must know the truth of it far, far better than my words could say. Is it to be the same thing over again—always over again? Self, first and last, the only consideration? Everything to please yourself; nothing from higher motives? God forgive you, Rose!"

"Oh, hush, hush! it is unkind—it is cruel. I would die for you if that would do any good!" cried Rose.

"These are easy words to say; for dying would do no good, neither would it be asked of you," said Mrs. Damerel impatiently. "Rose, I do not ask this in ordinary obedience, as a mother may command a child. It is not a child but a woman who must make such a decision; but it is my duty to show you your duty, and what is best for yourself as well as for others. No one—neither man nor woman, nor girl nor boy—can escape from duty to others; and when it is neglected some one must pay the penalty. But you—you are happier than most. You can, if you please, save your family."

"We are not starving, mamma," said Rose, with trembling lips; "we have enough to live upon—and I could work—I would do anything"—

"What would your work do, Rose? If you could teach—and I don't think you could teach—you might earn enough for your own dress; that would be all. Oh, my dear! listen to me. The little work a girl can do is nothing. She can make a sacrifice of her own inclination—of her fancy but as for work, she has nothing in her power."

"Then I wish there were no girls!" cried Rose, as many a poor girl has done before her, "if we can do nothing but be a burden—if there is no work for us, no use for us, but only to sell ourselves. Oh, mamma, mamma! do you know what you are asking me to do?"

"I know a great deal better than you do, or you would not repeat to me this vulgar nonsense about selling yourself. Am I likely to bid you sell yourself? Listen to me, Rose. I want you to be happy, and so you would be—nay, never shake your head at me—you would be happy with a man who loves you, for you would learn to love him. Die for us! I have heard such words from the lips of people who would not give up a morsel of their own will—not a whim, not an hour's comfort"—

"But I—I am not like that," cried Rose, stung to the heart. "I would give up anything—everything—for the children and you!"

"Except what you are asked to give up; except the only thing which you can give up. Again I say, Rose, I have known such cases. They are not rare in this world."

"Oh, mamma, mamma!"

"You think I am cruel. If you knew my life, you would not think so; you would understand my fear and horror of this amiable self-seeking which looks so natural. Rose," said her mother, dropping into a softer tone, "I have something more to say to you—perhaps something that will weigh more with you than anything I can say. Your father had set his heart on this. He spoke to me of it on his death-bed. God knows! perhaps he saw then what a dreary struggle I should have, and how little had been done to help us through. One of the last things he said to me was, 'Incledon will look after the boys.'"

"Papa said that?" said Rose, putting out her hands to find a prop. Her limbs seemed to refuse to support her. She was unprepared for this new, unseen antagonist. "Papa? How did he know?"

The mother was trembling and pale, too, overwhelmed by the recollection as well as by her anxiety to conquer. She made no direct answer to Rose's question, but took her hand within both of hers, and continued, with her eyes full of tears: "You would like to please *him*, Rose—it was almost the last thing he said—to please him, and to rescue me from anxieties I can see no end to, and to secure Bertie's future. Oh, Rose! you should thank God that you can do so much for those you love. And you would be happy, too. You are young, and love begets love. He would do everything that man could do to please you. He is a good man, with a kind heart; you would get to love him; and, my dear, you would be happy, too."

"Mamma," said Rose, with her head bent down and some silent tears dropping upon Mr. Incledon's flowers—a flush of color came over her downcast face, and then it grew pale again; her voice sounded so low that her mother stooped towards her to hear what she said—"mamma, I should like to tell you something."

Mrs. Damerel made an involuntary movement—a slight instinctive withdrawal from the confidence. Did she guess what it was? If she did so, she made up her mind at the same time not to know it. "What is it, dear?" she said tenderly but quickly. "Oh, Rose! do you think I don't understand your objections? But, my darling, surely you may trust your mother, who loves you more than all the world. You will not reject it—I know you will not reject it. There is no blessing that is not promised to those that deny themselves. He will not hurry nor press you, dear. Rose, say I may give him a kind answer when he comes?"

Rose's head was swimming, her heart throbbing in her ears and her throat. The girl was not equal to such a strain. To have the living and the dead both uniting against her—both appealing to her in the several names of love and duty against love—was more than she could bear. She had sunk into the nearest chair, unable to stand, and she no longer felt strong enough, even had her mother been willing to hear it, to make that confession which had been on her lips. At what seemed to be the extremity of human endurance, she suddenly saw one last resource in which she might still find safety, and grasped at it, scarcely aware what she did. "May I see Mr. Incledon myself if he comes?" she gasped, almost under her breath.

"Surely, dear," said her mother, surprised; "of course that would be the best—if you are able for it, if you will think well before you decide, if you will promise to do nothing hastily. Oh, Rose! do not break my heart!"

"It is more likely to be my own that I will break," said the girl, with a shadow of a smile passing over her face. "Mamma, will you be very kind, and say no more? I will think, think—everything that you say; but let me speak to him myself, if he comes."

Mrs. Damerel looked at her very earnestly, half suspicious, half sympathetic. She went up to her softly and put her arms round her, and pressed the girl's drooping head against her breast. "God bless you, my darling!" she said, with her eyes full of tears; and kissing her hastily, went out of the room, leaving Rose alone with her thoughts.

If I were to tell you what these thoughts were, and all the confusion of them, I should require a year to do it. Rose had no heart to stand up and fight for herself all alone against the world. Her young frame ached and trembled from head to foot with the unwonted strain. If there had been indeed any one—any one—to struggle for; but how was she to stand alone and battle for herself? Everything combined against her; every motive, every influence. She sat in a vague trance of pain, and, instead of thinking over what had been said, only saw visions gleaming before her of the love which was a vision, nothing more, and which she was called upon to resign. A vision—that was all; a dream, perhaps, without any foundation. It seemed to disperse like a mist, as the world melted and dissolved around her—the world which she had known—showing a new world, a dreamy, undiscovered country, forming out of darker vapors before her. She sat thus till the stir of the children in the house warned her that they had come in from their daily walk to the early dinner. She listened to their voices and noisy steps and laughter with the strangest feeling that she was herself a dreamer, having nothing in common with the fresh, real life where all the voices rang out so clearly, where people said what they meant with spontaneous outcries and laughter, and there was no concealed meaning and nothing beneath the sunny surface; but when she heard her mother's softer tones speaking to the children, Rose got up hurriedly, and fled to the shelter of her room. If anything more were said to her she thought she must die. Happily Mrs. Damerel did not know that it was her voice, and not the noise of the children, which was too much for poor Rose's over-strained nerves. She sent word by Agatha that Rose must lie down for an hour and try to rest; and that quiet was the best thing for her headache, which, of course, was the plea the girl put forth to excuse her flight and seclusion. Agatha, for her part, was very sorry and distressed that Rose should miss her dinner, and wanted much to bring something up-stairs for her, which was at once the kindest and most practical suggestion of all.

The bustle of dinner was all over and the house still again in the dreary afternoon quiet, when Agatha, once more, with many precautions, stole into the room. "Are you awake?" she said; "I hope your head is better. Mr. Incledon is in the drawing-room, and mamma says, please, if you are better will you go down, for she is busy; and you are to thank him for the grapes and for the flowers. What does Mr. Incledon want, coming so often? He was here only yesterday, and sat for hours with mamma. Oh! what a ghost you look, Rose! Shall I bring you some tea?"

"It is too early for tea. Never mind; my head is better."

"But you have had no dinner," said practical Agatha; "it is not much wonder that you are pale."

Rose did not know what she answered, or if she said anything. Her head seemed to swim more than ever. Not only was it all true about Mr. Incledon, but she was going to talk to him, to decide her own fate finally one way or other. What a good thing that the drawing-room was so dark in the afternoon that he could not remark how woe-begone she looked, how miserable and pale!

He got up when she came in, and went up to her eagerly, putting out his hands. I suppose he took her appearance as a proof that his suit was progressing well; and, indeed, he had come to-day with the determination to see Rose, whatever might happen. He took her hand into both of his, and for one second pressed it fervently and close. "It is very kind of you to see me. How can I thank you for giving me this opportunity?" he said.

"Oh, no! not kind; I wished it," said Rose, breathlessly, withdrawing her hand as hastily as he had taken it; and then, fearing her strength, she sat down in the nearest chair, and said, falteringly, "Mr. Incledon, I wanted very much to speak to you myself."

"And I, too," he said—her simplicity and eagerness thus opened the way for him and saved him all embarrassment—"I, too, was most anxious to see you. I did not venture to speak of this yesterday, when I met you. I was afraid to frighten and distress you; but I have wished ever since that I had dared"—

"Oh, please do not speak so!" she cried. In his presence Rose felt so young and childish, it seemed impossible to believe in the extraordinary change of positions which his words implied.

"But I must speak so. Miss Damerel, I am very conscious of my deficiencies by your side—of the disparity between us in point of age and in many other ways; you, so fresh and untouched by the world, I affected by it, as every man is more or less; but if you will commit your happiness to my hands, don't think, because I am not so young as you, that I will watch over it less carefully—that it will be less precious in my eyes."

"Ah! I was not thinking of my happiness," said Rose; "I suppose I have no more right to be happy than other people—but oh! if you would let me speak to you! Mr. Incledon, oh! why should you want me? There are so many girls better, more like you, that would be glad. Oh! what is there in me? I am silly; I am not well educated, though you may think so. I am not clever enough to be a companion you would care for. I think it is because you don't know."

Mr. Incledon was so much taken by surprise that he could do nothing but laugh faintly at this strange address. "I was not thinking either of education or of wisdom, but of you,—only you," he said.

"But you know so little about me; you think I must be nice because of papa; but, papa himself was never satisfied with me. I have not read very much. I know very little. I am not good for anywhere but home. Mr. Incledon, I am sure you are deceived in me. This is what I wanted to say. Mamma does not see it in the same light; but I feel sure that you are deceived, and take me for something very different from what I am," said Rose, totally unconscious that every word she said made Mr. Incledon more and more sure that he had done the very thing he ought to have done, and that he was not deceived.

"Indeed, you mistake me altogether," he said. "It is not merely because you are a piece of excellence—it is because I love you, Rose."

"Love me! Do you love me?" she said, looking at him with wondering eyes; then drooping with a deep blush under his gaze—"but I—do not love you."

"I did not expect it; it would have been too much to expect; but if you will let me love you, and show you how I love you, dear!" said Mr. Incledon, going up to her softly, with something of the tenderness of a father to a child, subduing the eagerness of a lover. "I don't want to frighten you; I will not hurry nor tease; but some time you might learn to love me."

"That is what mamma says," said Rose, with a heavy sigh.

Now this was scarcely flattering to a lover. Mr. Incledon felt for the moment as if he had received a downright and tolerably heavy blow; but he was in earnest, and prepared to meet with a rebuff or two. "She says truly," he answered, with much gravity. "Rose,—may I call you Rose?—do not think I will persecute or pain you; only do not reject me hastily. What I have to say for myself is very simple. I love you—that is all; and I will put up with all a man may for the chance of winning you, when you know me better, to love me in return."

These were almost the same words as those Mrs. Damerel had employed; but how differently they sounded; they had not touched Rose's heart at all before; but they did now with a curious mixture of agitation and terror, and almost pleasure. She was sorry for him, more than she could have thought possible, and somehow felt more confidence in him, and freedom to tell him what was in her heart.

"Do not answer me now, unless you please," said Mr. Incledon. "If you will give me the right to think your family mine, I know I can be of use to them. The boys would become my charge, and there is much that has been lost which I could make up had I the right to speak to your mother as a son. It is absurd, I know," he said, with a half-smile; "I am about as old as she is; but all these are secondary questions. The main thing is—you. Dear Rose, dear child, you don't know what love is"—

"Ah!" the girl looked up at him suddenly, her countenance changing. "Mr. Incledon, I have not said all to you that I wanted to say. Oh, do not ask me any more! Tell mamma that you have given it up! or I must tell you something that will break my heart."

"I will not give it up so long as there is any hope," he said; "tell me—what is it? I will do nothing to break your heart."

She made a pause. It was hard to say it, and yet, perhaps, easier to him than it would be to face her mother and make this tremendous confession. She twisted her poor little fingers together in her bewilderment and misery, and fixed her eyes upon them as if their interlacing were the chief matter in hand. "Mr. Incledon," she said, very low, "there was some one else—oh, how can I say it!—some one—whom I cared for—whom I can't help thinking about."

"Tell me," said Mr. Incledon, bravely quenching in his own mind a not very amiable sentiment; for it seemed to him that if he could but secure her confidence all would be well. He took her hand with caressing gentleness, and spoke low, almost as low as she did. "Tell me, my darling; I am your friend, confide in me. Who was it? May I know?"

"I cannot tell you who it was," said Rose, with her eyes still cast down, "because he has never said anything to me; perhaps he does not care for me; but this has happened: without his ever asking me, or perhaps wishing it, I cared for him. I know a girl should not do so, and that is why I cannot—cannot! But," said Rose raising her head with more confidence, though still reluctant to meet his eye, "now that you know this you will not think of me any more, Mr. Incledon. I am so sorry if it makes you at all unhappy; but I am of very little consequence; you cannot be long unhappy about me."

"Pardon me if I see it in quite a different light," he said. "My mind is not at all changed. This is but a fancy. Surely a man who loves you, and says so, should be of more weight than one of whose feelings you know nothing."

"I know about my own," said Rose, with a little sigh; "and oh, don't think, as mamma does, that I am selfish! It is not selfishness; it is because I know, if you saw into my heart, you would not ask me. Oh, Mr. Incledon, I would die for them all if I could! but how could I say one thing to you, and mean another? How could I let you be deceived?"

"Then, Rose, answer me truly; is your consideration solely for me?"

She gave him an alarmed, appealing look, but did not reply.

"I am willing to run the risk," he said, with a smile, "if all your fear is for me; and I think you might run the risk too. The other is an imagination; I am real, very real," he added, "very constant, very patient. So long as you do not refuse me absolutely, I will wait and hope."

Poor Rose, all her little art was exhausted. She dared not, with her mother's words ringing in her ears, and with all the consequences so clearly before her, refuse him absolutely, as he said. She had appealed to him to withdraw, and he would not withdraw. She looked at him as if he were the embodiment of fate, against which no man can strive.

"Mr. Incledon," she said, gravely and calmly, "you would not marry any one who did not love you?"

"I will marry you, Rose, if you will have me, whether you love me or not," he said; "I will wait for the love, and hope."

"Oh, be kind!" she said, driven to her wits' end. "You are free, you can do what you please, and there are so many girls in the world besides me. And I cannot do what I please," she added, low, with a piteous tone, looking at him. Perhaps he did not hear these last words. He turned from her with I know not what mingling of love, and impatience, and wounded pride, and walked up and down the darkling room, making an effort to command himself. She thought she had moved him at last, and sat with her hands clasped together, expecting the words which would be deliverance to her. It was almost dark, and the firelight glimmered through the low room, and the dim green glimmer of the twilight crossed its ruddy rays, not more unlike than the two who thus stood so strangely opposed to each other. At last, Mr. Incledon returned to where Rose sat in the shadow, touched by neither one illumination nor the other, and eagerly watching him as he approached her through the uncertain gleams of the ruddy light.

"There is but one girl in the world for me," he said, somewhat hoarsely. "I do not pretend to judge for any one but myself. So long as you do not reject me, I will hope."

And thus their interview closed. When he had got over the disagreeable shock of encountering that indifference on the part of the woman he loved, which is the greatest blow that can be given to a man's vanity, Mr. Incledon was not at all down-hearted about the result. He went away with half a dozen words to Mrs. Damerel, begging her not to press his suit, but to let the matter take its course. "All will go well if we are patient," he said, with a composure which, perhaps, surprised her; for women are apt to prefer the hot-headed in such points, and Mrs. Damerel did not reflect that, having waited so long, it was not so hard on the middle-aged lover to wait a little longer. But his forbearance at least was of immediate service to Rose, who was allowed time to recover herself after her agitation, and had no more exciting appeals addressed to her for some time. But Mr. Incledon went and came, and a soft, continued pressure, which no one could take decided objection to, began to make itself felt.

CHAPTER XII.

Mr. Incledon went and came; he did not accept his dismissal, nor, indeed, had any dismissal been given to him. A young lover, like Edward Wodehouse, would have been at once crushed and rendered furious by the appeal Rose had made so ineffectually to the man of experience who knew what he was about. If she was worth having at all, she was worth a struggle; and Mr. Incledon, in the calm exercise of his judgment, knew that at the last every good thing falls into the arms of the patient man who can wait. He had not much difficulty in penetrating the thin veil which she had cast over the "some one" for whom she cared, but who, so far as she knew, did not care for her. It could be but one person, and the elder lover was glad beyond description to know that his rival had not spoken, and that he was absent and likely to be absent. Edward Wodehouse being thus disposed of, there was no one else in Mr. Incledon's way, and with but a little patience he was sure to win.

As for Rose, though she felt that her appeal had been unsuccessful, she too was less discouraged by it than she could have herself supposed. In the first place she was let alone; nothing was pressed upon her; she had time allowed her to calm down, and with time everything was possible. Some miracle would happen to save her; or, if not a miracle, some ordinary turn of affairs would take the shape of miracle, and answer the same purpose. What is Providence, but a divine agency to get us out of trouble, to restore happiness, to make things pleasant for us? so, at least, one thinks when one is young; older, we begin to learn that Providence has to watch over many whose interests are counter to ours as well as our own; but at twenty, all that is good and necessary in life seems always on our side, and there seems no choice for Heaven but to clear the obstacles out of our way. Something would happen, and all would be well again; and Rose's benevolent fancy even exercised itself in finding for "poor Mr. Incledon" some one who would suit him better than herself. He was very wary, very judicious, in his treatment of her. He ignored that one scene when he had refused to give up his proposal, and conducted himself for some time as if he had sincerely given up his proposal, and was no more than the family friend, the most kind and sympathizing of neighbors. It was only by the slowest degrees that Rose found out that he had given up nothing, that his constant visits and constant attentions were so many meshes of the net in which her simple feet were being caught. For the first few weeks, as I have said, she was relieved altogether from everything that looked like persecution. She heard of him, indeed, constantly, but only in the pleasantest way. Fresh flowers came, filling the dim old rooms with brightness; and the gardener from Whitton came to look after the flowers and to suggest to Mrs. Damerel improvements in her garden, and how to turn the hall, which was large in proportion to the house, into a kind of conservatory; and baskets of fruit came, over which the children rejoiced; and Mr. Incledon himself came, and talked to Mrs. Damerel and played with them, and left books, new books, all fragrant from the printing, of which he sometimes asked Rose's opinion casually. None of all these good things was for her, and yet she had the unexpressed consciousness, which was pleasant enough so long as no one else remarked it and no recompense was asked, that but for her those pleasant additions to the family life would not have been. Then it was extraordinary how often he would meet them by accident in their walks, and how much trouble he would take to adapt his conversation to theirs, finding out (but this Rose did not discover till long after) all her tastes and likings. I suppose that having once made up his mind to take so much trouble, the pursuit of this shy creature, who would only betray what was in her by intervals, who shut herself up like the mimosa whenever she was too boldly touched, but who opened secretly with an almost childlike confidence when her fears were lulled to rest, became more interesting to Mr. Incledon than a more ordinary wooing, with a straightforward "yes" to his proposal at the end of it, would have been. His vanity got many wounds both by Rose's unconsciousness and by her shrinking; but he pursued his plan undaunted by either, having made up his mind to win her and no other; and the more difficult the fight was, the more triumphant would be the success.

This state of affairs lasted for some time; indeed, everything went on quietly, with no apparent break in the gentle monotony of existence at the White House, until the spring was so far advanced as to have pranked itself out in a flood of primroses. It was something quite insignificant and incidental which for the first time reawakened Rose's fears. He had looked at her with something in his eyes which betrayed him, or some word had dropped from his lips which startled her; but the first direct attack upon her peace of mind did not come from Mr. Incledon. It came from two ladies on the Green, one of whom at least was very innocent of evil meaning. Rose was walking with her mother on an April afternoon, when they met Mrs. Wodehouse and Mrs. Musgrove, likewise taking their afternoon walk. Mrs. Musgrove was a very quiet person, who interfered with nobody, yet who was mixed up with everything that went on on the Green, by right of being the most sympathetic of souls, ready to hear everybody's grievance and to help in everybody's trouble. Mrs. Wodehouse struck straight across the Green to meet Mrs. Damerel and Rose, when she saw them, so that it was by no ordinary chance meeting, but an encounter sought eagerly on one side at least, that this revelation came. Mrs. Wodehouse was full of her subject, vibrating, with it to the very flowers on her bonnet, which thrilled and nodded against the blue distance like a soldier's plumes. She came forward with a forced exuberance of cordiality, holding out both her hands.

"Now tell me!" she said; "may we congratulate you? Is the embargo removed? Quantities of people have assured me that we need not hold our tongues any longer, but that it is all settled at last."

"What is all settled at last?" asked Mrs. Damerel, with sudden stiffness and coldness. "I beg your pardon, but I really don't in the least know what you mean."

"I said I was afraid you were too hasty," said Mrs. Musgrove.

"Well, if one can't believe the evidence of one's senses, what is one to believe?" cried Mrs. Wodehouse. "It is not kind, Rose, to keep all your old friends so long in suspense. Of course, it is very easy to see on which side the hesitation is; and I am sure I am very sorry if I have been premature."

"You are more than premature," said Mrs. Damerel with a little laugh, and an uneasy color on her cheek, "for you are speaking a language neither Rose nor I understand. I hope, Mrs. Wodehouse, you have good news from your son."

"Oh, very good news indeed!" said the mother, whose indignation on her son's behalf made the rose on her bonnet quiver: and then there were a few further interchanges, of volleys in the shape of questions and answers of the most civil description, and the ladies shook hands and parted. Rose had been struck dumb altogether by the dialogue, in which, trembling and speechless, she had taken no part. When they had gone on for a few yards in silence, she broke down in her effort at self-restraint.

"Mamma, what does she mean?"

"Oh, Rose, do not drive me wild with your folly!" said Mrs. Damerel. "What could she mean but one thing? If you think for one moment, you will have no difficulty in understanding what she means."

Rose woke up, as a sick man wakes after a narcotic, feverish and trembling. "I thought," she said, slowly, her heart beginning to throb, and her head to ache in a moment—"I thought it was all given up."

"How could you think anything so foolish? What symptom can you see of its having been given up? Has he ceased coming? Has he ceased trying to please you, ungrateful girl that you are? Indeed you go too far for ordinary patience; for it cannot be stupidity—you are not stupid," said Mrs. Damerel, excitedly; "you have not even that excuse."

"Oh, mamma, do not be angry!" said poor Rose; "I thought—it seemed so natural that, as he saw more of me, he would give it up. Why should he care for me? I am not like him, nor fit to be a great lady; he must see that."

"This is false humility, and it is very ill timed," said Mrs. Damerel. "Strange though it may seem, seeing more of you does not make him give it up; and if you are too simple or too foolish to see how much he is devoted to you, no one else is. Mrs. Wodehouse had a spiteful meaning, but she is not the first who has spoken to me. All our friends on the Green believe, like her, that everything is settled between you; that it is only some hesitation about—about our recent sorrow which keeps it from being announced."

Rose turned upon her mother for the first time with reproach in her eyes. "You should have told me!" she said, with momentary passion; "you ought to have told me,—for how was I to know?"

"Rose, I will not allow such questions; you are not a fool nor a child. Did you think Mr. Incledon came for me? or Agatha, perhaps? He told you he would not give you up. You were warned what his object was—more than warned. Was I to defeat my own wishes by keeping you constantly on your guard? You knew what he wanted, and you have encouraged him and accepted his attentions."

"I—encouraged him?"

"Whenever a girl permits, she encourages," said Mrs. Damerel, with oracular solemnity. "In matters of this kind, Rose, if you do not refuse at once, you commit yourself, and sooner or later you must accept."

"You never told me so before. Oh, mamma! how was I to know? you never said this to me before."

"There are things that one knows by intuition," said Mrs. Damerel; "and, Rose, you know what my opinion has been all along. You have no right to refuse. On the one side, there is everything that heart can desire; on the other, nothing but a foolish, childish disinclination. I don't know if it goes so far as disinclination; you seem now to like him well enough."

"Do you not know the difference?" said Rose, turning wistful eyes upon her mother. "Oh, mamma, you who ought to know so much better than I do! I *like* him very well—what does that matter?"

"It matters everything; liking is the first step to love. You can have no reason, absolutely no reason, for refusing him if you like him. Rose, oh, how foolish this is, and what a small, what a very small place there seems to be in your mind for the thought of duty! You tell us you are ready to die for us—which is absurd—and yet you cannot make up your mind to this!"

"It is different," said Rose; "oh, it is different! Mamma, listen a moment; you are a great deal better than I am; you love us better than we love each other; you are never tired of doing things for us; whether you are well or whether you are ill it does not matter; you are always ready when the children want you. I am not blind," said the girl, with tears. "I know all you do and all you put up with; but, mamma, you who are good, you who know how to deny yourself, would *you* do this?"

"Rose!"

"Would you do it?" cried Rose, excited and breathless, pursuing her advantage.

Mrs. Damerel was not old, nor was life quenched in her either by her years or her sorrows. Her face flushed, under her heavy widow's veil, all over, with a violent overwhelming blush like a girl's.

"Rose," she said, passionately, "how dare you—how dare you put such a question to your mother? I do it!—either you are heartless altogether, or you are mad, and don't know what you say."

"Forgive, me mamma; but, oh, let me speak! There is nothing else so hard, nothing so disagreeable, but you would do it for us; but you would not do this. There is a difference, then? you do not deny it now?"

"You use a cruel argument," said Mrs. Damerel, the blush still warm upon her matron cheek, "and it is not a true one. I am your father's wife. I am your mother and Bertie's, who are almost man and woman. All my life would be reversed, all my relations confused, if I were to make such a sacrifice; besides, it is impossible," she said, suddenly; "I did not think that a child of mine would ever have so insulted me."

"I do not mean it for insult, mamma. Oh, forgive me! I want you only to see the difference. It is not like anything else. You would do anything else, and so would I; but, oh, not this! You see it yourself—not this, mamma."

"It is foolish to attempt to argue with you," said Mrs. Damerel; and she hurried in, and up-stairs to her room, leaving Rose, not less excited, to follow. Rose had scarcely calculated upon the prodigious force of her own argument. She was half frightened by it, and half ashamed of having used it, yet to some extent triumphant in her success. There was quite a bank of flowers in the hall as she passed through—flowers which she stopped to look at and caress, with little touches of fondness as flower-lovers use, before she recollected that they were Mr. Incledon's flowers. She took up a book which was on the hall table, and hurried on to avoid that contemplation, and then she remembered that it was Mr. Incledon's book. She was just entering the drawing-room as she did so, and threw it down pettishly on a chair by the door; and, lo! Mr. Incledon himself rose, a tall shadow against the window, where he had been waiting for the ladies' return.

"Mamma has gone up-stairs; I will call her," said Rose, with confusion, turning away.

"Nay, never mind; it is a pity to disturb Mrs. Damerel, and it is long, very long, since you have allowed me a chance of talking to you."

"Indeed, we see each other very often," said Rose, falteringly.

"Yes, I see you in a crowd, protected by the children, or with your mother, who is my friend, but who cannot help me—I wanted to ask about the book you threw down so impatiently as you came in. Don't you like it?" said Mr. Incledon, with a smile.

What a relief it was! She was so grateful to him for not making love to her, that I almost think she would have consented to marry him, had he asked her, before he left that evening. But he was very cautious and very wise, and, though he had come with no other intention, he was warned by the excitement in her looks, and stopped the very words on her lips, for which Rose, short-sighted, like all mortals, was very thankful to him, not knowing how much the distinct refusal, which it was in her heart to give, would have simplified all their affairs.

This, however, was at once the first and the last of Rose's successes. When she saw traces of tears about her mother's eyes, and how pale she was, her heart smote her, and she made abject submission of herself, and poured out her very soul in excuses, so that Mrs. Damerel, though vanquished for the moment, took higher ground after it. The mother, indeed, was so much shaken by the practical application of her doctrines, that she felt there was no longer time for the gradual undermining which was Mr. Incledon's policy. Mrs. Damerel did not know what reply she could make if Rose repeated her novel and strenuous argument, and felt that now safety lay in as rapid a conclusion of the matter as possible; so that from this moment every day saw the closing of the net over poor Rose. The lover became more close in his attendance, the mother more urgent in her appeals; but so cleverly did he manage the matter that his society was always a relief to the girl when hard driven, and she gradually got to feel herself safer with him, which was a great deal in his favor. Everything, however, went against Rose. The ladies on the Green made gentle criticisms upon her, and called her a sly little puss. Some hoped she would not forget her humble friends when she came into her kingdom; some asked her what she meant by dragging her captive so long at her chariot wheels; and the captive himself, though a miracle of goodness, would cast pathetic looks at her, and make little speeches full of meaning. Rose began to feel herself like a creature at bay; wherever she turned she could see no way of escape; even sharp-eyed Agatha, in the wisdom of fifteen, turned against her.

"Why don't you marry Mr. Incledon, and have done with it?" said Agatha. "I would, if I were you. What a good thing it would be for you! and I suppose he would be kind to the rest of us, too. Why, you would have your carriage—two or three carriages, and a horse to ride, and you might go abroad if you liked, or do anything you liked. How I should like to have quantities of money, and a beautiful house, and everything in the world I wanted! I should not shilly-shally like you."

"No one has everything in the world they want," said Rose, solemnly, thinking also, if Mr. Incledon had been "some one else" how much easier her decision would have been.

"You seem to think they do," said Agatha, "or you would not make such a fuss about Mr. Incledon. Why, what do you object to? I suppose it's because he is not young enough. I think he is a very nice man, and very good-looking. I only wish he had asked me."

"Agatha, you are too young to talk of such things," said Rose, with the dignity of her seniority.

"Then I wish my eldest sister was too young to put them into my head," said Agatha.

This conversation drove Rose from her last place of safety, the schoolroom, where hitherto she had been left in quiet. A kind of despair seized her. She dared not encounter her mother in the drawing-room, where probably Mr. Incledon also would appear towards the twilight. She put on her hat and wandered out, her heart full of a subdued anguish, poignant yet not unsweet, for the sense of intense suffering is in its way a kind of excitement and painful enjoyment to the very young. It was a spring afternoon, soft and sweet, full of promise of the summer, and Rose, quite unused to walking or indeed doing anything else alone, found a certain pleasure in the loneliness and silence. How tranquillizing it was to be alone; to have no one near who would say anything to disturb her; nobody with reproachful eyes; nothing around or about but the soft sky, the trees growing green, the grass which waved its thin blades in the soft air! It seemed to Rose that she was out for a long time, and that the silence refreshed her, and made her strong for her fate whatever it might be. Before she returned home she went in at the old familiar gate of the rectory, and skirted the lawn by a by-path she knew well, and stole down the slope to the little platform under the old May-tree. By this time it had begun to get dark; and as Rose looked across the soft undulations of the half visible country, every line of which was dear and well known to her, her eyes fell suddenly upon a gleam of light from among the trees. What friendly sprite had lighted the lights so early in the parlor of the cottage at Ankermead, I cannot tell, but they glimmered out from the brown clump of trees and took Rose so by surprise that her eyes filled with sudden moisture, and her heart beat with a muffled throbbing in her ears. So well she recollected the warm summer evening long ago (and yet it was not a year ago), and every word that was said. "Imagination will play me many a prank before I forget this night!" Did he mean that? had he forgotten it? or was he perhaps leaning over the ship's side somewhere while the big vessel rustled through the soft broad sea, thinking of home, as he had said, seeing the lights upon the coast, and dreaming of his mother's lighted windows, and of that dim, dreamy, hazy landscape, so soft and far inland, with the cottage lamp shining out from that brown clump of trees? The tears fell softly from Rose's eyes through the evening dimness which hid them almost from herself; she was very sad, heart-broken—and yet not so miserable as she thought. She did not know how long she sat there, looking at the cottage lights through her tears. The new rector and his wife sat down to dinner all unaware of the forlorn young visitor who had stolen into the domain which was now theirs, and Rose's mother began to get sadly uneasy about her absence, with a chill dread lest she should have pressed her too far and driven her to some scheme of desperation. Mr. Incledon came out to look for her, and met her just outside the rectory gate, and was very kind to her, making her take his arm and leading her gently home without asking a question.

"She has been calling at the rectory, and I fear it was too much for her," he said; an explanation which made the quick tears start to Mrs. Damerel's own eyes, who kissed her daughter and sent her up-stairs without further question. I almost think Mr. Incledon was clever enough to guess the true state of affairs; but he told this fib with an admirable air of believing it, and made Rose grateful to the very bottom of her heart.

Gratitude is a fine sentiment to cultivate in such circumstances. It is a better and safer beginning than that pity which is said to be akin to love. Rose struggled no more after this. She surrendered quietly, made no further resistance, and finally yielded a submissive assent to what was asked of her. She became "engaged" to Mr. Incledon, and the engagement was formally announced, and all the Green joined in with congratulations, except, indeed, Mrs. Wodehouse, who called in a marked manner just after the ladies had been seen to go out, and left a huge card, which was all her contribution to the felicitations of the neighborhood. There was scarcely a lady in the parish except this one who did not take the trouble to walk or drive to the White House and kiss Rose and congratulate her mother. "Such a very excellent match—everything that a mother could desire!" they said. "But you must get a little more color in your cheeks, my dear," said old Lady Denvil. "This is not like the dear rector's Rose in June. It is more like a pale China rose in November." What could Rose do but cry at this allusion? It was kind of the old lady (who was always kind), to give her this excellent reason and excuse for the tears in her eyes.

And then there came, with a strange, hollow, far-off sound, proposals of dates and days to be fixed, and talk about the wedding dresses and the wedding tour. She listened to it all with an inward shiver; but, fortunately for Rose, Mrs. Damerel would hear of no wedding until after the anniversary of her husband's death, which had taken place in July. The

Green discussed the subject largely, and most people blamed her for standing on this punctilio; for society in general, with a wise sense of the uncertainty of all human affairs, has a prejudice against the postponement of marriages which it never believes in thoroughly till they have taken place. They thought it ridiculous in a woman of Mrs. Damerel's sense, and one, too, who ought to know how many slips there are between the cup and the lip; but Mr. Incledon did not seem to object, and, of course, everybody said no one else had a right to interfere.

All this took place in April, when the Damerels had been but three months in their new house. Even that little time had proved bitterly to them many of the evils of their impoverished condition, for already Mr. Hunsdon had begun to write of the long time Bertie had been at school, and the necessity there was that he should exert himself; and even Reginald's godfather, who had always been so good, showed signs of a disposition to launch his charge, too, on the world, suggesting that perhaps it might be better, as he had now no prospect of anything but working for himself, that he should leave Eton. Mrs. Damerel kept these humiliations to herself, but it was only natural that they should give fire to her words in her arguments with Rose; and it could not be denied that the family had spent more than their income permitted in the first three months. There had been the mourning, and the removal, and so many other expenses, to begin with. It is hard enough to struggle with bills as Mrs. Damerel had done in her husband's lifetime, when by means of the wisest art and never-failing attention it was always possible to pay them as they became urgent; but when there is no money at all, either present or in prospect, what is a poor woman to do? They made her sick many a time when she opened the drawer in her desk and looked at them. Even with all she could accept from Mr. Incledon (and that was limited by pride and delicacy in many ways), and with one less to provide for, Mrs. Damerel would still have care sufficient to make her cup run over. Rose's good fortune did not take her burden away.

Thus things went on through the early summer. The thought of Rose's trousseau nearly broke her mother's heart. It must be to some degree in consonance with her future position, and it must not come from Mr. Incledon; and where was it to come from? Mrs. Damerel had begun to write a letter to her brother, appealing, which it was a bitter thing to do, for his help, one evening early in May. She had written after all her children had left her, when she was alone in the old-fashioned house, where all the old walls and the old stairs uttered strange creaks and jars in the midnight stillness, and the branches of the creepers tapped ghostly taps against the window. Her nerves were over-strained, and her heart was sore, notwithstanding her success in the one matter which she had struggled for so earnestly; and after writing half her letter Mrs. Damerel had given it up, with a strange feeling that something opposed the writing of it, some influence which she could not define, which seemed to stop her words, and made her incapable of framing a sentence. She gave it up with almost a superstitious thrill of feeling, and a nervous tremor which she tried in vain to master; and, leaving it half-written in her blotting-book, stole up-stairs to bed in the silence, as glad to get out of the echoing, creaking room as if it had been haunted. Rose heard her come up-stairs, and thought with a little bitterness as she lay awake, her pillow wet with the tears which she never shed in the daylight, of her mother's triumph over her, and how all this revolution was her work. She heard something like a sigh as her mother passed her door, and wondered almost contemptuously what she could have to sigh about, for Rose felt all the other burdens in the world to be as nothing in comparison with her burden; as, indeed we all do.

Next morning, however, before Rose was awake, Mrs. Damerel came into her room in her dressing-gown, with her hair, which was still so pretty, curling about her shoulders, and her face lit up with a wonderful pale illumination like a northern sky.

"What is it?" cried Rose, springing up from her bed.

"Rose," said Mrs. Damerel, gasping for breath, "we are rich again! No! it is impossible—but it is true; here it is in this letter—my uncle Ernest is dead, and he has left us all his money. We are richer than ever I was in all my life."

Rose got up, and ran and kissed her mother, and cried, with a great cry that rang all over the house, "Then I am free!"

CHAPTER XIII.

There is no such picturesque incident in life as the sudden changes of fortune which make a complete revolution in the fate of families or individuals without either action or merit of their own. That which we are most familiar with is the change from comfort to poverty, which so often takes place, as it had done with the Damerels, when the head of a house, either incautious or unfortunate, goes out of this world, leaving not only sorrow but misery behind him, and the bereavement is intensified by social downfall and all the trials that accompany loss of means. But for the prospect of Mr. Incledon's backing up, this would have implied a total change in the prospects and condition of the entire household, for all hope of higher education must have been given up for the boys; they must have dropped into any poor occupation which happened to be within their reach, with gratitude that they were able to maintain themselves; and as for the girls, what could they do, poor children, unless by some lucky chance of marriage? This poor hope would have given them one remaining chance not possible to their brothers; but, except that, what had they all to look forward to? This was Mrs. Damerel's excuse for urging Rose's unwilling consent to Mr. Incledon's proposal. But lo! all this was changed as by a magician's wand. The clouds rolled off the sky, the sunshine came out again, the family recovered its prospects, its hopes, its position, its freedom, and all this in a moment. Mrs. Damerel's old uncle Edward had been an original who had quarrelled with all his family. She had not seen him since she was a child, and none of her children had seen him at all—and she never knew exactly what it was that made him select her for his heir. Probably it was pity; probably admiration for the brave stand she was making against poverty—perhaps only caprice, or because she had never asked anything from him; but, whatever the cause was, there was the happy result. In the evening anxiety, care, discouragement, bitter humiliation, and pain; in the morning sudden ease, comfort, happiness—for, in the absence of anything better, it is a great happiness to have money enough for all your needs, and to be able to give your children what they want, and pay your bills and owe no man anything. In the thought of being rich enough to do all this Mrs. Damerel's heart leapt up in her breast, like the heart of a child. Next moment she remembered, and with a pang of sudden anguish asked herself, oh, why—why had not this come sooner, when *he*, who would have enjoyed it so much, might have had the enjoyment? This feeling, sprang up by instinct in her mind, notwithstanding her bitter consciousness of all she had suffered from her husband's carelessness and self-regard—for love is the strangest of all sentiments, and can indulge and condemn in a breath, without any sense of inconsistency. This was the pervading thought in Mrs. Damerel's mind as the news spread through the awakened house, making even the children giddy with hopes of they knew not what. How *he* would have enjoyed it all—the added luxury, the added consequence! far more than she would have enjoyed it, notwithstanding that it came to her like life to the dying. She had taken no notice of Rose's exclamation, nor of the flush of joy which the girl betrayed. I am not sure, indeed, that she observed them, being absorbed in her own feelings, which come first even in the most generous minds, at such a crisis and revolution of fate.

As for Rose, it was the very giddiness of delight that she felt, unreasoning and even unfeeling. Her sacrifice had become unnecessary—she was free! So she thought, poor child, with a total indifference to honor and her word which I do not attempt to excuse. She never once thought of her word, or of the engagement she had come under, or of the man who had been so kind to her, and loved her so faithfully. The children had holiday on that blessed morning, and Rose ran out with them into the garden, and ran wild with pure excess of joy. This was the first day that Mr. Nolan had visited them since he went to his new duties, and as the curate came into the garden, somewhat tired after a long walk, and expecting to find his friends something as he had left them—if not mourning, yet subdued as true mourners continue after the sharpness of their grief is ended—he was struck with absolute dismay to meet Rose, flushed and joyous, with one of the children mounted on her shoulders, and pursued by the rest, in the highest of high romps, the spring air resounding with their shouts. Rose blushed a little when she saw him. She put down her little brother from her shoulder, and came forward beaming with happiness and kindness.

"Oh, how glad I am that you have come to-day," she said, and explained forthwith all the circumstances with the frank diffuse explanatoriness of youth. "Now we are rich again; and oh, Mr. Nolan, I am so happy!" she cried, her soft eyes glowing with an excess of light which dazzled the curate.

People who have never been rich themselves, and never have any chance of being rich, find it difficult sometimes to understand how others are affected in these unwonted circumstances. He was confounded by her frank rapture, the joy which seemed to him so much more than was necessary.

"I'm glad to see you so happy," he said, bewildered; "no doubt money's a blessing, and ye've felt the pinch, my poor child, or ye wouldn't be so full of your joy."

"Oh, Mr. Nolan, how I have felt it!" she said, her eyes filling with tears. A cloud fell over her face for the space of a moment, and then she laughed and cried out joyously, "but thank Heaven that is all over now."

Mrs. Damerel was writing in the drawing-room, writing to her boys to tell them the wonderful news. Rose led the visitor in, pushing open the window which opened on the garden. "I have told him all about it, and how happy we are," she said, going up to her mother with all the confidence of happiness, and giving her, with unwonted demonstration, a kiss upon her forehead, before she danced out again to the sunny garden. Mrs. Damerel was a great deal more sober in her exultation, which relieved the curate. She told him how it had all come about, and what a deliverance it was; then cried a little, having full confidence in his sympathy, over that unremovable regret that it had not come sooner. "How happy it would have made him—and relieved all his anxiety about us," she said. Mr. Nolan made some inarticulate sound, which she took for assent; or, at least, which it pleased her to mistake for assent. In her present mood it was sweet to think that her husband had been anxious, and the curate knew human nature too well to contradict her. And then she gave him a little history of the past three months during which he had been absent, and of Rose's engagement and all Mr. Incledon's good qualities. "He would have done anything for us," said Mrs. Damerel;

"but oh, how glad I am we shall not want anything—only Rose's happiness, which in his hands is secure."

"Mr. Incledon!" said the curate, with a little wonder in his voice. "Ah, and so that is it. I thought it couldn't be nothing but money that made the child so pleased."

"You thought she looked very happy?" said the mother, with a sudden fright.

"Happy! she looked like her name—nothing is so happy as that but the innocent creatures of God; and sure I did her injustice thinking 'twas the money," the curate said, with mingled compunction and wonder; for the story altogether sounded very strange to him, and he could not but marvel at the thought that Mr. Incledon's love, once so evidently indifferent to her, should light such lamps of joy now in Rose's eyes.

Mrs. Damerel changed the subject abruptly. A mist of something like care came over her face. "I have had a great deal of trouble and much to think about since I saw you," she said; "but I must not enter upon that now that it is over. Tell me about yourself."

He shrugged his shoulders as he told her how little there was to tell. A new parish, with other poor folk much like those he had left, and other rich folk not far dissimilar—the one knowing as little about the other as the two classes generally do. "That is about all my life is ever likely to be," he said, with a half smile, "between the two, with no great hold on either. I miss Agatha, and Dick, and little Patty—and you to come and talk to most of all," he said, looking at her with an affectionate wistfulness which went to her heart. Not that Mr. Nolan was "in love" with Mrs. Damerel, as vulgar persons would say, laughing; but the loss of her house and society was a great loss to the middle-aged curate, never likely to have a house of his own.

"We must make it up as much as we can by talking all day long now you are here," she said, with kind smiles; but the curate, though he was fond of her, was quick to see that she avoided the subject of Mr. Incledon, and was ready to talk of anything rather than that; though, indeed, the first love and first proposed marriage in a family has generally an interest exceeding everything else to the young heroine's immediate friends.

They had the merriest dinner at two o'clock, according to the habit of their humility, with roast mutton, which was the only joint Mary Jane could not spoil; simple fare, which contented the curate as well as a French chef could have done. He told them funny stories of his new people, at which the children shouted with laughter, and described the musical parties at the vicarage, and the solemn little dinners, and all the dreary entertainments of a small town. The White House had not heard so much innocent laughter, so many pleasant foolish jokes, for years—and I don't think that Rose had ever so distinguished herself in the domestic circle. She had been generally considered too old for fun among the children—too dignified, more on mamma's side—giving herself up to poetry and other such solemn occupations; but to-day the suppressed fountain burst forth. Even Mrs. Damerel did not escape the infection of that laughter which rang like silver bells. The deep mourning they all wore, the poor little rusty black frocks trimmed still with crape, perhaps reproached the laughter now and then; but fathers and mothers cannot expect to be mourned for a whole year, and, indeed, the rector, to these little ones at least, had not been much more than a name.

"Rose," said Mrs. Damerel, when the meal was over, and they had returned into the drawing-room, "I think we had better arrange to go up to town one of these days to see about your things. I have been putting off, and putting off, on account of our poverty; but it is full time to think of your trousseau now."

Rose stood still as if she had been suddenly struck by some mortal blow. She looked at her mother with eyes opening wide, lips falling apart, and a sudden deadly paleness coming over her face. From the fresh sweetness of that rose tint which had come back to her she became all at once ashy-gray, like an old woman. "My—what, mamma?" she faltered, putting her hands upon the table to support herself. "I—did not hear—what you said."

"You'll find me in the garden, ladies, when you want me," said the curate, with a man's usual cowardice, "bolting" as he himself expressed it, through the open window.

Mrs. Damerel looked up from where she had seated herself at the table, and looked her daughter in the face.

"Your trousseau," she said, calmly, "what else should it be?"

Rose gave a great and sudden cry. "That's all over, mamma, all over, isn't it?" she said, eagerly; then hastening round to her mother's side, fell on her knees by her chair, and caught her hand and arm, which she embraced and held close to her breast. "Mamma! speak to me—it's all over—all over! You said the sacrifices we made would be required no longer. It is not needed any more, and it's all over. Oh, say so, with your own lips, mamma!"

"Rose, are you mad?" said her mother, drawing away her hand; "rise up, and do not let me think my child is a fool. Over! Is honor over, and the word you have pledged, and the engagement you have made?"

"Honor!" said Rose, with white lips; "but it was for you I did it, and you do not require it any more."

"Rose," cried Mrs. Damerel, "you will drive me distracted. I have often heard that women have no sense of honor, but I did not expect to see it proved in your person. Can you go and tell the man who loves you that you will not marry him because we are no longer beggars? He would have helped us when we were penniless—is that a reason for casting him off now?"

Rose let her mother's hand go, but she remained on her knees by the side of the chair, as if unable to move, looking up in Mrs. Damerel's face with eyes twice their usual size.

"Then am I to be none the better—none the better?" she cried piteously; "are they all to be saved, all rescued, except me?"

"Get up, Rose," said Mrs. Damerel impatiently, "and do not let me hear any more of this folly. Saved! from an excellent man who loves you a great deal better than you deserve—from a lot that a queen might envy—everything that is beautiful and pleasant and good! You are the most ungrateful girl alive, or you would not venture to speak so to me."

Rose did not make any answer. She did not rise, but kept still by her mother's side, as if paralyzed. After a moment Mrs. Damerel, in angry impatience, turned from her and resumed her writing, and there the girl continued to kneel, making no movement, heart-stricken, turned into marble. At length, after an interval, she pulled timidly at her mother's dress, looking at her with eyes so full of entreaty, that they forced Mrs. Damerel, against her will, to turn round and meet that pathetic gaze.

"Mamma," she said, under her breath, her voice having failed her, "just one word—is there no hope for me, can you do nothing for me? Oh, have a little pity! You could do something if you would but try."

"Are you mad, child?" cried the mother again—"do something for you? What can I do? You promised to marry him of your own will; you were not forced to do it. You told me you liked him not so long ago. How does this change the matter, except to make you more fit to be his wife? Are you mad?"

"Perhaps," said Rose softly; "if being very miserable is being mad, then I am mad, as you say."

"But you were not very miserable yesterday; you were cheerful enough."

"Oh, mamma, then there was no hope," cried Rose, "I had to do it—there was no help; but now hope has come—and must every one share it, every one get deliverance, but me?"

"Rose," said Mrs. Damerel, "when you are Mr. Incledon's wife every one of these wild words will rise up in your mind and shame you. Why should you make yourself unhappy by constant discussions? you will be sorry enough after for all you have allowed yourself to say. You have promised Mr. Incledon to marry him and you must marry him. If I had six times Uncle Ernest's money it would still be a great match for you."

"Oh, what do I care for a great match!"

"But I do," said Mrs. Damerel, "and whether you care or not has nothing to do with it. You have pledged your word and your honor, and you cannot withdraw from them. Rose, your marriage is fixed for the end of July. We must have no more of this."

"Three months," she said, with a little convulsive shudder. She was thinking that perhaps even yet something might happen to save her in so long a time as three months. "Not quite three months," said Mrs. Damerel, whose thoughts were running on the many things that had to be done in the interval. "Rose, shake off this foolish repining, which is unworthy of you, and go out to good Mr. Nolan, who must be dull with only the children. Talk to him and amuse him till I am ready. I am going to take him up to Whitton to show him the house."

Rose went out without a word; she went and sat down in the little shady summer-home where Mr. Nolan had taken refuge from the sun and from the mirth of the children. He had already seen there was something wrong, and was prepared with his sympathy: whoever was the offender Mr. Nolan was sorry for that one; it was a way he had; his sympathies did not go so much with the immaculate and always virtuous; but he was sorry for whosoever had erred or strayed, and was repenting of the same. Poor Rose—he began to feel himself Rose's champion, because he felt sure that it was Rose, young, thoughtless, and inconsiderate, who must be in the wrong. Rose sat down by his side with a heart-broken look in her face, but did not say anything. She began to beat with her fingers on the table as if she were beating time to a march. She was still such a child to him, so young, so much like what he remembered her in pinafores, that his heart ached for her. "You are in some little bit of trouble?" he said at last.

"Oh, not a little bit," cried Rose, "a great, very great trouble!" She was so full of it that she could not talk of anything else. And the feeling in her mind was that she must speak or die. She began to tell her story in the woody arbor with the gay noise of the children close at hand, but hearing a cry among them that Mr. Incledon was coming, started up and tied on her hat, and seizing Mr. Nolan's arm, dragged him out by the garden door. "I cannot see him to-day!" she cried, and led the curate away, dragging him after her to a quiet by-way over the fields in which she thought they would be safe. Rose had no doubt whatever of the full sympathy of this old friend. She was not afraid even of his disapproval. It seemed certain to her that he must pity at least if not help. And to Rose, in her youthful confidence in others, there was nothing in this world which was unalterable of its nature: no trouble, except death, which could not be got rid of by the intervention of friends.

It chilled her a little, however, as she went on, to see the curate's face grow longer and longer, graver and graver. "You should not have done it," he said, shaking his head, when Rose told him how she had been brought to give her consent.

"I know I ought not to have done it, but it was not my doing. How could I help myself? And now, oh, now, dear Mr. Nolan, tell me what to do! Will *you* speak to mamma? Though she will not listen to me she might hear you."

"But I don't see what your mamma has to do with it," said the curate. "It is not to her you are engaged—nor is it she who has given her word; you must keep your word, we are all bound to do that."

"But a great many people don't do it," said Rose, driven to the worst of arguments by sheer despair of her cause.

"*You* must," said Mr. Nolan: "the people who don't are not people to be followed. You have bound yourself and you must stand by it. He is a good man and you must make the best of it. To a great many it would not seem hard at all. You have accepted him, and you must stand by him. I do not see what else can be done now."

"Oh, Mr. Nolan, you speak as if I were married, and there was no hope."

"It is very much the same thing," said the curate; "you have given your word. Rose, you would not like to be a jilt; you must either keep your word or be called a jilt—and called truly. It is not a pleasant character to have."

"But it would not be true!"

"I think it would be true. Mr. Incledon, poor man, would have good reason to think so. Let us look at it seriously, Rose. What is there so very bad in it that you should do a good man such an injury? He is not old. He is very agreeable and very rich. He would make you a great lady, Rose."

"Mr. Nolan, do you think I care for that?"

"A great many people care for it, and so do all who belong to you. Your poor father wished it. It had gone out of my mind, but I can recollect very well now; and your mother wishes it—and for you it would be a great thing, you don't know how great. Rose, you must try to put all this reluctance out of your mind, and think only of how many advantages it has."

"I care nothing, for the advantages," said Rose, "the only one thing was for the sake of the others. He promised to be good to the boys and to help mamma; and now we don't need his help any more."

"A good reason, an admirable reason," cried the curate with unwonted sarcasm, "for casting him off now. Few people state it so frankly, but it is the way of the world."

Rose gave him a look so full of wondering that the good man's heart was touched. "Come," he said, "you had made up your mind to it yesterday. It cannot be so very bad after all. At your age nothing can be very bad, for you can always adapt yourself to what is new. So long as there's nobody else in the way that's more to your mind," he said, turning upon her with a penetrating glance.

Rose said nothing in reply. She put up her hands to her face, covering it, and choking the cry which came to her lips. How could she to a man, to one so far separated from love and youth as was Mr. Nolan, make this last confession of all?

The curate went away that night with a painful impression on his mind. He did not go to Whitton, as Mrs. Damerel had promised, to see Rose's future home, but he saw the master of it, who, disappointed by the headache with which Rose had retreated to her room, on her return from her walk with the curate, did not show in his best aspect. None of the party indeed did; perhaps the excitement and commotion of the news had produced a bad result—for nothing could be flatter or more deadly-lively than the evening which followed. Even the children were cross and peevish, and had to be sent to bed in disgrace; and Rose had hidden herself in her room, and lines of care and irritation were on Mrs. Damerel's forehead. The great good fortune which had befallen them did not, for the moment at least, bring happiness in its train.

CHAPTER XIV.

ROSE did not go down-stairs that night. She had a headache, which is the prescriptive right of a woman in trouble. She took the cup of tea which Agatha brought her, at the door of her room, and begged that mamma would not trouble to come to see her, as she was going to bed. She was afraid of another discussion, and shrank even from seeing any one. She had passed through a great many different moods of mind in respect to Mr. Incledon, but this one was different from all the rest. All the softening of feeling of which she had been conscious died out of her mind; his very name became intolerable to her. That which she had proposed to do, as the last sacrifice a girl could make for her family, an absolute renunciation of self and voluntary martyrdom for them, changed its character altogether when they no longer required it. Why should she do what was worse than death, when the object for which she was willing to die was no longer before her; when there was, indeed, no need for doing it at all? Would Iphigenia have died for her word's sake, had there been no need for her sacrifice? and why should Rose do more than she? In this there was, the reader will perceive, a certain change of sentiment; for though Rose had made up her mind sadly and reluctantly to marry

Mr. Incledon, yet she had not thought the alternative worse than death. She had felt while she did it the ennobling sense of having given up her own will to make others happy, and had even recognized the far-off and faint possibility that the happiness which she thus gave to others might, some time or other, rebound upon herself. But the moment her great inducement was removed, a flood of different sentiment came in. She began to hate Mr. Incledon, to feel that he had taken advantage of her circumstances, that her mother had taken advantage of her, that every one had used her as a tool to promote their own purpose, with no more consideration for her than had she been altogether without feeling. This thought went through her mind like a hot breath from a furnace, searing and scorching everything. And now that their purpose was served without her, she must still make this sacrifice—for honor! For honor! Perhaps it is true that women hold this motive more lightly than men, though indeed the honor that is involved in a promise of marriage does not seem to influence either sex very deeply in ordinary cases. I am afraid poor Rose did not feel its weight at all. She might be forced to keep her word, but her whole soul revolted against it. She had ceased to be sad and resigned. She was rebellious and indignant, and a hundred wild schemes and notions began to flit through her mind. To jump in such a crisis as this from the tender resignation of a martyr for love into the bitter and painful resistance of a domestic rebel who feels that no one loves her, is easy to the young mind in the unreality which more or less envelops everything to youth. From the one to the other was but a step. Yesterday she had been the centre of all the family plans, the foundation of comfort, the chief object of their thoughts. Now she was in reality only Rose the eldest daughter, who was about to make a brilliant marriage, and therefore was much in the foreground, but no more loved or noticed than any one else. In reality this change had actually come, but she imagined a still greater change; and fancy showed her to herself as the rebellious daughter, the one who had never fully done her duty, never been quite in sympathy with her mother, and whom all would be glad to get rid of, in marriage or any other way, as interfering with the harmony of the house. Such of us as have been young may remember how easy these revolutions of feeling were, and with what quick facility we could identify ourselves as almost adored or almost hated, as the foremost object of everybody's regard or an intruder in everybody's way. Rose passed a very miserable night, and the next day was, I think, more miserable still. Mrs. Damerel did not say a word to her on the subject which filled her thoughts, but told her that she had decided to go to London in the beginning of the next week, to look after the "things" which were necessary. As they were in mourning already, there was no more trouble of that description necessary on Uncle Ernest's account, but only new congratulations to receive, which poured in on every side.

"I need not go through the form of condoling, for I know you did not have much intercourse with him, poor old gentleman," one lady said; and another caught Rose by both hands and exclaimed on the good luck of the family in general.

"Blessings, like troubles, never come alone," she said. "To think you should have a fortune tumbling down upon you on one side, and on the other this chit of a girl carrying off the best match in the country!"

"I hope we are sufficiently grateful for all the good things Providence sends us," said Mrs. Damerel, fixing her eyes severely upon Rose.

Oh, if she had but had the courage to take up the glove thus thrown down to her! But she was not yet screwed up to that desperate pitch.

Mr. Incledon came later, and in his joy at seeing her was more lover-like than he had yet permitted himself to be.

"Why, I have not seen you since this good news came!" he cried, fondly kissing her in his delight and heartiness of congratulation, a thing he had never done before. Rose broke from him and rushed out of the room, white with fright and resentment.

"Oh, how dared he! how dared he!" she cried, rubbing the spot upon her cheek which his lips had touched with wild exaggeration of dismay.

And how angry Mrs. Damerel was! She went up-stairs after the girl, and spoke to her as Rose had never yet been spoken to in all her soft life— upbraiding her with her heartlessness, her disregard of other people's feelings, her indifference to her own honor and pledged word. Once more Rose remained up-stairs, refusing to come down, and the house was aghast at the first quarrel which had ever disturbed its decorum.

Mr. Incledon went away bewildered and unhappy, not knowing whether to believe that this was a mere ebullition of temper, such as Rose had never shown before, which would have been a venial offence, rather amusing than otherwise to his indulgent fondness; or whether it meant something more, some surging upwards of the old reluctance to accept him, which he had believed himself to have overcome. This doubt chilled him to the heart, and gave him much to think of as he took his somewhat dreary walk home—for failure, after there has been an appearance of success, is more discouraging still than when there has been no opening at all in the clouded skies. And Agatha knocked at Rose's locked door, and bade her good night through the keyhole with a mixture of horror and respect—horror for the wickedness, yet veneration for the courage which could venture thus to beard all constituted authorities. Mrs. Damerel herself said no good night to the rebel. She passed Rose's door steadily without allowing herself to be led away by the impulse which tugged at her heart to go in and give the kiss of grace, notwithstanding the impenitent condition of the offender. Had the mother done this, I think all that followed might have been averted, and that Mrs. Damerel would have been able eventually to carry out her programme and arrange the girl's life as she wished. But she thought it right to show her displeasure, though her heart almost failed her.

Rose had shut herself up in wild misery and passion. She had declared to herself that she wanted to see no one; that she would not open her door, nor subject herself over again to such reproaches as had been poured upon her. But yet when she heard her mother pass without even a word, all the springs of the girl's being seemed to stand still. She could not believe it. Never before in all her life had such a terrible occurrence taken place. Last night, when she had gone to bed to escape remark, Mrs. Damerel had come in ere she went to her own room and asked after the pretended headache, and kissed her, and bade her keep quite still and be better to-morrow. Rose got up from where she was sitting, expecting her mother's appeal and intending to resist, and went to the door and put her ear against it and listened. All was quiet. Mrs. Damerel had gone steadily along the corridor, had entered the rooms of the other children, and now shut her own door—sure signal that the day was over. When this inexorable sound met her ears, Rose crept back again to her seat and wept bitterly, with an aching and vacancy in her heart which it is beyond words to tell. It seemed to her that she was abandoned, cut off from the family love, thrown aside like a waif and stray, and that things would never be again as they had been. This terrible conclusion always comes in to aggravate the miseries of girls and boys. Things could never mend, never again be as they had been. She cried till she exhausted herself, till her head ached in dire reality, and she was sick and faint with misery and the sense of desolation; and then wild schemes and fancies came into her mind. She could not bear it—scarcely for those dark helpless hours of the night could she bear it—but must be still till daylight; then, poor forlorn child, cast off by every one, abandoned even by her mother, with no hope before her but this marriage, which she hated, and no prospect but wretchedness—then she made up her mind she would go away. She took out her little purse and found a few shillings in it, sufficient to carry her to the refuge which she had suddenly thought of. I think she would have liked to fly out of sight and ken and hide herself forever, or at least until all who had been unkind to her had broken their hearts about her, as she had read in novels of unhappy heroines doing. But she was too timid to take such a daring step, and she had no money, except the ten shillings in her poor little pretty purse, which was not meant to hold much. When she had made up her mind, as she thought, or to speak more truly, when she had been quite taken possession of by this wild purpose, she put a few necessaries into a bag to be ready for her flight, taking her little prayer-book last of all, which she kissed and cried over with a heart wrung with many pangs. Her father had given it her on the day she was nineteen—not a year since. Ah, why was not she with him, who always understood her, or why was not he here? He would never have driven her to such a step as this. He was kind, whatever any one might say of him. If he neglected some things, he was never hard upon any one—at least, never hard upon Rose—and he would have understood her now. With an anguish of sudden sorrow, mingled with all the previous misery in her heart, she kissed the little book and put it into her bag. Poor child! it was well for her that her imagination had that sad asylum at least to take refuge in, and that the rector had not lived long enough to show how hard in worldliness a soft and self-indulgent man can be.

Rose did not go to bed. She had a short, uneasy sleep, against her will, in her chair—dropping into constrained and feverish slumber for an hour or so in the dead of the night. When she woke, the dawn was blue in the window, making the branches of the honeysuckle visible through the narrow panes. There was no sound in heaven or earth except the birds chirping, but the world seemed full of that; for all the domestic chat has to be got over in all the nests before men awake and drown the delicious babble in harsher commotions of their own. Rose got up and bathed her pale face and red eyes, and put on her hat. She was cold, and glad to draw a shawl round her and get some consolation and strength from its warmth; and then she took her bag in her hand, and opening her door, noiselessly stole out. There was a very early train which passed the Dingle station, two miles from Dinglefield, at about five o'clock, on its way to London; and Rose hoped, by being in time for that, to escape all pursuit. How strange it was, going out, like a thief into the house, all still and shut up, with its windows closely barred, the shutters up, and a still, unnatural half-light gleaming in through the crevices! As she stole downstairs her very breathing, the sound of her own steps, frightened Rose; and when she looked in at the open door of the drawing-room and saw all the traces of last night's peaceful occupations, a strange feeling that all the rest were dead and she a fugitive stealing guiltily away, came on her so strongly that she could scarcely convince herself it was not true. It was like the half-light that had been in all the rooms when her father lay dead in the house, and made her shiver. Feeling more and more like a thief, she opened the fastenings of the hall door, which were rusty and gave her some trouble. It was difficult to open them, still more difficult to close it softly without alarming the house; and this occupied her mind, so that she made the last step almost without thinking what she was doing. When she had succeeded in shutting the door, then it suddenly flashed upon her, rushed upon her like a flood—the consciousness of what she had done. She had left home, and all help and love and protection; and—Heaven help her!—here she was out of doors in the open-eyed day, which looked at her with a severe, pale calm—desolate and alone! She held by the pillars of the porch to support her for one dizzy, bewildered moment; but now was not the time to break down or let her terrors, her feelings overcome her. She had taken the decisive step and must go on now.

Mrs. Damerel, disturbed perhaps by the sound of the closing door, though she did not make out what it was, got up and looked out from the window in the early morning, and, at the end of the road which led to the Green, saw a solitary figure walking, which reminded her of Rose. She had half forgotten Rose's perverseness, in her sleep, and I think the first thing that came into her mind had been rather the great deliverance sent to her in the shape of uncle Ernest's fortune, than the naughtiness—though it was almost too serious to be called naughtiness—of her child. And though it struck her for the moment with some surprise to see the slim young figure on the road so early, and a passing notion crossed her mind that something in the walk and outline was like Rose, yet it never occurred to her to connect that unusual appearance with her daughter. She lay down again when she had opened the window, with a little half-wish, half-prayer, that Rose might "come to her senses" speedily. It was too early to get up and though Mrs. Damerel could not sleep, she had plenty to think about and this morning leisure was the best time for it. Rose prevailed largely among her subjects of thoughts, but did not fill her whole mind. She had so many other children, and so much to consider about them all!

Meanwhile Rose went on to the station, like a creature in a dream, feeling the very trees, the very birds watch her, and wondering that no faces peeped at her from the curtained cottage windows. How strange to think that all the people were asleep, while she walked along through the dreamy world, her footsteps filling it with strange echoes! How fast and soundly it slept, that world, though all the things out-of-doors were in full movement, interchanging their opinions, and taking council upon all their affairs! She had never been out, and had not very often been awake, at such an early hour, and the stillness from all human sounds and voices, combined with the wonderful fulness of the language of Nature, gave her a strange bewildered feeling, like that a traveller might have in some strange star or planet peopled with beings different from man. It seemed as if all the human inhabitants had resigned, and given up their places to another species. The fresh air which blew in her face, and the cheerful stir of the birds, recovered her a little from the fright with which she felt herself alone in that changed universe—and the sight of the first wayfarer making his way, like herself, towards the station, gave her a thrill of pain, reminding her that she was neither walking in a dream nor in another planet, but on the old-fashioned earth, dominated by men, and where she shrank from being seen or recognized. She put her veil down over her face as she stole in, once more feeling like a thief, at the wooden gate. Two or three people only, all of the working class, were kicking their heels on the little platform. Rose took her ticket with much trepidation, and stole into the quietest corner to await the arrival of the train. It came up at last with a great commotion, the one porter rushing to open the door of a carriage, out of which, Rose perceived quickly, a gentleman jumped, giving directions about some luggage. An arrival was a very rare event at so early an hour in the morning. Rose went forward timidly with her veil over her face to creep into the carriage which this traveller had vacated, and which seemed the only empty one. She had not looked at him, nor had she any curiosity about him. The porter, busy with the luggage, paid no attention to her, for which she was thankful, and she thought she was getting away quite unobserved, which gave her a little comfort. She had her foot on the step, and her hand on the carriage door, to get in.

"Miss Damerel!" cried an astonished voice close by her ear.

Rose's foot failed on the step. She almost fell with the start she gave. Whose voice was it? a voice she knew—a voice somehow that went to her heart; but in the first shock she did not ask herself any questions about it, but felt only the distress and terror of being recognized. Then she decided that it was her best policy to steal into the carriage to escape questions. She did so, trembling with fright; but as she sat down in the corner, turned her face unwittingly towards the person, whoever it was, who had recognized her. He had left his luggage, and was gazing at her with his hand on the door. His face, all flushed with delight, gleamed upon her like sudden sunshine. "Miss Damerel!" he cried again, "you here at this hour?"

"Oh, hush! hush!" she cried, putting up her hand with instinctive warning. "I—don't want to be seen."

I am not sure that she knew him at the first glance. Poor child, her heart was too deeply preoccupied to do more than flutter feebly at the sight of him, and no secondary thought as to how he had come here, or what unlooked-for circumstance had brought him back, was within the range of her intelligence. Edward Wodehouse made no more than a momentary pause ere he decided what to do. He slipped a coin into the porter's ready hand, and gave him directions about his luggage. "Keep it safe till I return; don't send it home. I am obliged to go to town for an hour or two," he said, and sprang again into the carriage he had just left. His heart was beating with no feeble flutter. He had the promptitude of a man who knows that no opportunity ought to be neglected. The door closed upon them with that familiar bang which we all know so well; the engine shrieked, the wheels jarred, and Rose Damerel and Edward Wodehouse —two people whom even the Imperial Government of England had been moved to separate—moved away into the distance, as if they had eloped with each other, sitting face to face.

Her heart fluttered feebly enough—his heart as strong as the pulsations of the steam-engine, and he thought almost as audible; but the first moment was one of embarrassment. "I cannot get over the wonder of this meeting," he said. "Miss Damerel, what happy chance takes you to London this morning of all others? Some fairy must have done it for me?"

"No happy chance at all," said Rose, shivering with painful emotion, and drawing her shawl closer round her. What could she say to him?—but she began to realize that it was *him*, which was the strangest, bewildering sensation. As for him, knowing of no mystery and no misery, the tender sympathy in his face grew deeper and deeper. Could it be poverty? could she be going to work like any other poor girl? A great throb of love and pity went through the young man's heart.

"Don't be angry with me," he said; "but I cannot see you here, alone and looking sad—and take no interest. Can you tell me what it is? Can you make any use of me? Miss Damerel, don't you know there is nothing in the world that would make me so happy as to be of service to you?"

"Have you just come home?" she asked.

"This morning; I was on my way from Portsmouth. And you—won't you tell me something about yourself?"

Rose made a tremendous effort to go back to the ordinary regions of talk; and then she recollected all that had happened since he had been away. "You know that papa died," she said, the tears springing to her eyes with an effort of nature which relieved her brain and heart.

"I heard that: I was very, very sorry."

"And then for a time we were very poor; but now we are well off again by the death of mamma's uncle Ernest; that is all, I think," she said, with an attempt at a smile.

Then there was a pause. How was he to subject her to a cross-examination? and yet Edward felt that, unless something had gone very wrong, the girl would not have been here.

"You are going to town?" he said. "It is very early for you; and alone"—

"I do not mind," said Rose; and then she added quickly, "when you go back, will you please not say you have seen me? I don't want any one to know."

"Miss Damerel, something has happened to make you unhappy?"

"Yes," she said, "but never mind. It does not matter much to any one but me. Your mother is very well. Did she know that you were coming home?"

"No, it is quite sudden. I am promoted by the help of some kind unknown friend or another, and they could not refuse me a few days' leave."

"Mrs. Wodehouse will be very glad," said Rose. She seemed to rouse out of her preoccupation to speak to him, and then fell back. The young sailor was at his wits' end. What a strange coming home it was to him! He had dreamt of his first meeting with Rose in a hundred different ways, and rehearsed it, and all that he would say to her; but such a wonderful meeting as this had never occurred to him; and to have her entirely to himself, yet not to know what to say!

"There must be changes since I left. It will soon be a year ago," he said, in sheer despair.

"I do not remember any changes," said Rose, "except the rectory. We are in the White House now. Nothing else has happened that I know—yet."

This little word made his blood run cold—*yet*. Did it mean that something was about to happen? He tried to overcome that impression by a return to the ground he was sure of. "May I speak of last year?" he said. "I went away very wretched—as wretched as any man could be."

Rose was too far gone to think of the precautions with which such a conversation ought to be conducted. She knew what he meant, and why should she pretend she did not? Not that this reflection passed through her mind, which acted totally upon impulse, without any reflection at all.

"It was not my fault," she said, simply. "I was alone with papa, and he would not let me go."

"Ah!" he said, his eyes lighting up; "you did not think me presumptuous, then? you did not mean to crush me? Oh! if you knew how I have thought of it, and questioned myself! It has never been out of my mind for a day—for an hour"—

She put up her hand hastily. "I may be doing wrong," she said, "but it would be more wrong still to let you speak. They would think it was for this I came away."

"What is it? what is it?" he said; "something has happened. Why may not I tell you, when I have at last this blessed opportunity? Why is it wrong to let me speak?"

"They will think it was for this I came away," said Rose. "Oh! Mr. Wodehouse, you should not have come with me. They will say I knew you were to be here. Even mamma, perhaps, will think so, for she does not think well of me, as papa used to do. She thinks I am selfish, and care only for my own pleasure," said Rose with tears.

"You have come away without her knowledge?"

"Yes."

"Then you are escaping from some one?" said Wodehouse, his face flushing over.

"Yes! yes."

"Miss Damerel, come back with me. Nobody, I am sure, will force you to do anything. Your mother is too good to be unkind. Will you come back with me? Ah, you must not—you must not throw yourself upon the world; you do not know what it is," said the young sailor, taking her hand, in his earnestness. "Rose—dear Rose—let me take you back."

She drew her hand away from him, and dried the hot tears which scorched her eyes. "No, no," she said. "You do not know, and I want nobody to know. You will not tell your mother, nor any one. Let me go, and let no one think of me any more."

"As if that were possible!" he cried.

"Oh, yes, it is possible. I loved papa dearly; but I seldom think of him now. If I could die you would all forget me in a year. To be sure I cannot die; and even if I did, people might say that was selfish too. Yes, you don't know what things mamma says. I have heard her speak as if it were selfish to die,—escaping from one's duties; and I am escaping from my duties; but it can never, never be a duty to marry when you cannot—

What am I saying?" said poor Rose. "My head is quite light, and I think I must be going crazy. You must not mind what I say."

CHAPTER XV.

EDWARD WODEHOUSE reached Dinglefield about eleven o'clock, coming back from that strange visit to town. He felt it necessary to go to the White House before even he went to his mother, but he was so cowardly as to go round a long way so as to avoid crossing the Green, or exhibiting himself to public gaze. He felt that his mother would never forgive him did she know that he had gone anywhere else before going to her, and, indeed, I think Mrs. Wodehouse's feeling was very natural. He put his hat well over his eyes, but he did not, as may be supposed, escape recognition—and went on with a conviction that the news of his arrival would reach his mother before he did, and that he would have something far from delightful to meet with when he went home.

As for Mrs. Damerel, when she woke up in the morning to the fact that Rose was gone, her first feelings, I think, were more those of anger than of alarm. She was not afraid that her daughter had committed suicide, or run away permanently; for she was very reasonable, and her mind fixed upon the probabilities of a situation rather than on the violent catastrophes which might be possible. It was Agatha who first brought her the news, open-mouthed, and shouting the information, "Oh, mamma, come here, come here, Rose has run away!" so that every one in the house could hear.

"Nonsense, child! she has gone—to do something for me," said the mother on the spur of the moment, prompt to save exposure even at the instant when she received the shock.

"But, mamma," cried Agatha, "her bed has not been slept in, her things are gone—her"—

Here Mrs. Damerel put her hand over the girl's mouth, and with a look she never forgot went with her into the empty nest, from which the bird had flown. All Mrs. Damerel's wits rallied to her on the moment to save the scandal which was inevitable if this were known. "Shut the door," she said in a low quiet voice. "Rose is very foolish: because she thinks she has quarrelled with me, to make such a show of her undutifulness! She has gone up to town by the early train."

"Then you knew!" cried Agatha, with eyes as wide open as just now her mouth had been.

"Do you think it likely she would go without my knowing?" said her mother; an unanswerable question, for which Agatha, though her reason discovered the imposture, could find no ready response. She looked on with wonder while her mother, with her own hands, tossed the coverings off the little white bed, and gave it the air of having been slept in. It was Agatha's first lesson in the art of making things appear as they are not.

"Rose has been foolish; but I don't choose that Mary Jane should make a talk about it, and tell everybody that she did not go to bed last night like a Christian—and do you hold your tongue," said Mrs. Damerel.

Agatha followed her mother's directions with awe, and was subdued all day by a sense of the mystery; for why, if mamma knew all about it, and it was quite an ordinary proceeding, should Rose have gone to town by the early train?

Mrs. Damerel, however, had no easy task to get calmly through the breakfast, and arrange her household matters for the day, with this question perpetually recurring to her, with sharp thrills and shoots of pain —Where was Rose? She had been angry at first, deeply annoyed and vexed, but now other feelings struck in. An anxiety, which did not suggest any definite danger, but was dully and persistently present in her mind, like something hanging over her, took possession of her whole being. Where had she gone? What could she be doing at that moment? What steps could her mother take to find out, without exposing her foolishness to public gaze? How should she satisfy Mr. Incledon? how conceal this strange disappearance from her neighbors? They all took what people are pleased to call "a deep interest" in Rose, and, indeed, in all the late rector's family; and Mrs. Damerel knew the world well enough to be aware that the things which one wishes to be kept secret, are just those which everybody manages to hear. She forgot even to be angry with Rose in the deep necessity of concealing the extraordinary step she had taken; a step enough to lay a young girl under an enduring stigma all her life; and what could she do to find her without betraying her? She could not even make an inquiry without risking this betrayal. She could not ask a passenger on the road, or a porter at the station, if they had seen her, lest she should thereby make it known that Rose's departure had been clandestine. All through the early morning, while she was busy with the children and the affairs of the house, this problem was working in her mind. Of all things this was the most important, not to compromise Rose, or to let any one know what a cruel and unkind step she had taken. Mrs. Damerel knew well how such a stigma clings to a girl, and how ready the world is to impute other motives than the real one. Perhaps she had been hard upon the child, and pressed a hateful sacrifice upon her unduly, but now Rose's credit was the first thing she thought of. She would not even attempt to get relief to her own anxiety at the cost of any animadversion upon Rose; or suffer anybody to suspect her daughter in order to ease herself. This necessity made her position doubly difficult and painful, for, without compromising Rose, she did not know how to inquire into her disappearance or what to do; and, as the moments passed over with this perpetual undercurrent going on in her mind, the sense of painful anxiety grew stronger and stronger. Where could she have gone? She had left no note, no letter behind her, as runaways are generally supposed to do. She had, her mother knew, only a few shillings in her purse; she had no relations at hand with whom she could find refuge. Where had she gone? Every minute this question pressed more heavily upon her, and sounded louder and louder. Could she go on shutting it up in her mind, taking counsel of no one? Mrs. Damerel felt this to be impossible, and after breakfast sent a telegram to Mr. Nolan, begging him to come to her "on urgent business." She felt sure that Rose had confided some of her troubles at least to him; and he was a friend upon whose help and secrecy she could fully rely.

Her mind was in this state of intense inward perturbation and outward calm, when, standing at her bedroom window, which commanded the road and a corner of the Green, upon which the road opened, she saw Edward Wodehouse coming towards the house. I suppose there was never any one yet in great anxiety and suspense, who did not go to the window with some sort of forlorn hope of seeing something to relieve them. She recognized the young man at once, though she did not know of his arrival, or even that he was looked for; and the moment she saw him instantly gave him a place—though she could not tell what place—in the maze of her thoughts. Her heart leaped up at sight of him, though he might be but walking past, he might be but coming to pay an ordinary call on his return, for anything she knew. Instinctively, her heart associated him with her child. She watched him come in through the little shrubbery, scarcely knowing where she stood, so intense was her suspense; then went down to meet him, looking calm and cold, as if no anxiety had ever clouded her firmament. "How do you do, Mr. Wodehouse? I did not know you had come back," she said, with perfect composure, as if he had been the most every-day acquaintance, and she had parted from him last night.

He looked at her with a countenance much paler and more agitated than her own, and, with that uneasy air of deprecation natural to a man who has a confession to make. "No one did; or, indeed, does," he said, "not even my mother. I got my promotion quite suddenly, and insisted upon a few days' leave to see my friends before I joined my ship."

"I congratulate you," said Mrs. Damerel, putting heroic force upon herself. "I suppose, then, I should have said Captain Wodehouse? How pleased your mother will be!"

"Yes," he said, abstractedly. "I should not, as you may suppose, have taken the liberty to come here so early merely to tell you a piece of news concerning myself. I came up from Portsmouth during the night, and when the train stopped at this station—by accident—Miss Damerel got into the same carriage in which I was. She charged me with this note to give to you."

There was a sensation in Mrs. Damerel's ears as if some sluice had given way in the secrecy of her heart, and the blood was surging and swelling upwards. But she managed to smile a ghastly smile at him, and to take the note without further display of her feelings. It was a little twisted note written in pencil, which Wodehouse, indeed, had with much trouble persuaded Rose to write. Her mother opened it with fingers trembling so much that the undoing of the scrap of paper was a positive labor to her. She dropped softly into a chair, however, with a great and instantaneous sense of relief, the moment she had read these few pencilled words:—

"Mamma, I have gone to Miss Margetts'. I am very wretched, and don't know what to do. I could not stay at home any longer. Do not be angry. I think my heart will break."

Mrs. Damerel did not notice these pathetic words. She saw "Miss Margetts," and that was enough for her. Her blood resumed its usual current, her heart began to beat less violently. She felt, as she leant back in her chair, exhausted and weak with the agitation of the morning; weak as one only feels when the immediate pressure is over. Miss Margetts was the school-mistress with whom Rose had received her education. No harm to Rose, nor her reputation, could come did all the world know she was there. She was so much and instantaneously relieved, that her watchfulness over herself intermitted, and she did not speak for a minute or two. She roused herself up with a little start when she caught Wodehouse's eye gravely fixed upon her.

"Thanks," she said; "I am glad to have this little note, telling me of Rose's safe arrival with her friends in London. It was very good of you to bring it. I do not know what put it into the child's head to go by that early train."

"Whatever it was, it was very fortunate for me," said Edward. "As we had met by such a strange chance I took the liberty of seeing her safe to Miss Margetts' house."

"You are very good," said Mrs. Damerel; "I am much obliged to you;" and then the two were silent for a moment, eying each other like wrestlers before they close.

"Mrs. Damerel," said young Wodehouse, faltering, and brave sailor as he was, feeling more frightened than he could have said, "there is something more which I ought to tell you. Meeting her so suddenly, and remembering how I had been balked in seeing her before I left Dinglefield, I was overcome by my feelings, and ventured to tell Miss Damerel"—

"Mr. Wodehouse, my daughter is engaged to be married!" cried Mrs. Damerel, with sharp and sudden alarm.

"But not altogether—with her own will," he said.

"You must be mistaken," said the mother, with a gasp for breath. "Rose is foolish, and changes with every wind that blows. She cannot have intended to leave any such impression on your mind. It is the result, I suppose of some lovers' quarrel. As this is the case, I need not say that though under any circumstances, I should deeply have felt the honor you do her yet, in the present, the only thing I can do is to say good morning and many thanks. Have you really not seen your mother yet?"

"Not yet. I am going"—

"Oh go, please, go!" said Mrs. Damerel. "It was extremely kind of you to bring the note before going home, but your mother would never forgive me if I detained you; good-by. If you are here for a few days I may hope to see you before you go."

With these words she accompanied him to the door, smiling cordially as she dismissed him. He could neither protest against the dismissal nor linger in spite of it, to repeat the love-tale which she had stopped on his lips. Her apparent calm had almost deceived him, and but for a little quiver of her shadow upon the wall, a little clasping together of her hands, with Rose's letter in them, which nothing but the keenest observation could have detected, he could almost have believed in his bewilderment that Rose had been dreaming, and that her mother was quite cognizant of her flight, and knew where she was going and all about it. But, however that might be, he had to go, in a very painful maze of thought, not knowing what to think or to hope about Rose, and having a whimsical certainty of what must be awaiting him at home, had his mother heard, as was most likely, of his arrival, and that he had gone first to the White House. Fortunately for him, Mrs. Wodehouse had not heard it; but she poured into his reluctant ears the whole story of Mr. Incledon and the engagement, and of all the wonders with which he was filling Whitton in preparation for his bride.

"Though I think she treated you very badly, after encouraging you as she did, and leading you on to the very edge of a proposal—yet one can't but feel that she is a very lucky girl," said Mrs. Wodehouse. "I hope you will take care not to throw yourself in their way, my dear; though, perhaps, on the whole, it would be best to show that you have got over it entirely and don't mind who she marries. A little insignificant chit of a girl not worth your notice. There are as good fish in the sea, Edward—or better, for that matter."

"Perhaps you are right, mother," he said, glad to escape from the subject; and then he told her the mystery of his sudden promotion, and how he had struggled to get this fortnight's leave before joining his ship, which was in commission for China. Mrs. Wodehouse fatigued her brain with efforts to discover who it could be who had thus mysteriously befriended her boy; and as this subject drew her mind from the other, Edward was thankful enough to listen to her suggestions of this man who was dead, and that man who was at the end of the world. He had not an idea himself who it could be, and, I think, cherished a furtive hope that it was his good service which had attracted the notice of my lords; for young men are easily subject to this kind of illusion. But his mind, it maybe supposed, was sufficiently disturbed without any question of the kind. He had to reconcile Rose's evident misery in her flight, with her mother's calm acceptance of it as a thing she knew of; and to draw a painful balance between Mrs. Damerel's power to insist and command, and Rose's power of resistance; finally, he had the despairing consciousness that his leave was only for a fortnight, a period too short for anything to be decided on. No hurried settlement of the extraordinary imbroglio of affairs which he perceived dimly—no license, however special, would make it possible to secure Rose in a fortnight's time; and he was bound to China for three years! This reflection, you may well suppose, gave the young man enough to think of, and made his first day at home anything but the ecstatic holiday which a first day at home ought to be.

As for Mrs. Damerel, when she went into her own house, after seeing this dangerous intruder to the door, the sense of relief which had been her only conscious feeling up to this moment gave place to the irritation and repressed wrath which, I think, was very natural. She said to herself, bitterly, that as the father had been so the daughter was. They consulted their own happiness, their own feelings, and left her to make everything straight behind them. What did it matter what she felt? What was the good of her but to bear the burden of their self-indulgence?—to make up for the wrongs they did, and conceal the scandal? I am aware that in such a case, as in almost all others, the general sympathy goes with the young; but yet I think poor Mrs. Damerel had much justification for the bitterness in her heart. She wept a few hot tears by herself which nobody even knew of or suspected, and then she returned to the children's lessons and her daily business, her head swimming a little, and with a weakness born of past agitation, but subdued into a composure not feigned but real. For after all, everything can be remedied except exposure, she thought to herself; and going to Miss Margetts' showed at least a glimmering of common-sense on the part of the runaway, and saved all public discussion of the "difficulty" between Rose and her mother. Mrs. Damerel was a clergyman's wife—nay, one might say a clergywoman in her own person, accustomed to all the special decorums and exactitudes which those who take the duties of the caste to heart consider incumbent upon that section of humanity; but she set about inventing a series of fibs on the spot with an ease which I fear long practice and custom had given. How many fibs had she been compelled to tell on her husband's behalf?—exquisite little romances about his health and his close study, and the mental occupations which kept him from little necessary duties; although she knew perfectly well that his study was mere desultory reading, and his delicate health, self-indulgence. She had shielded him so with that delicate network of falsehood that the rector had gone out of the world with the highest reputation. *She* had all her life been subject to remark as rather a commonplace wife for such a man, but no one had dreamt of criticising him. Now she had the same thing to begin over again; and she carried her system to such perfection that she began upon her own family, as indeed in her husband's case she had always done, imbuing the children with a belief in his abstruse studies and sensitive organization, as well as the outer world.

"Rose has gone to pay Miss Margetts a visit," she said, at the early dinner. "I think a little change will do her good. I shall run up to town in a few days and see after her things."

"Gone to Miss Margetts'! I wonder why no one ever said so," cried Agatha, who was always full of curiosity. "What a funny thing, to go off on a visit without even saying a word!"

"It was settled quite suddenly," said the mother, with perfect composure. "I don't think she has been looking well for some days; and I always intended to go to town about her things."

"What a very funny thing," repeated Agatha, "to go off at five o'clock; never to say a word to any one—not even to take a box with her clothes, only that little black bag. I never heard of anything so funny; and to be so excited about it that she never went to bed."

"Do not talk nonsense," said Mrs. Damerel, sharply; "it was not decided till the evening before, after you were all asleep."

"But, mamma"—

"I think you might take some of this pudding down to poor Mary Simpson," said Mrs. Damerel, calmly; "she has no appetite, poor girl; and, Agatha, you can call at the postoffice, and ask Mrs. Brown if her niece has got a place yet. I think she might suit me as housemaid, if she has not got a place."

"Then, thank Heaven," said Agatha, diverted entirely into a new channel, "we shall get rid of Mary Jane!"

Having thus, as it were, made her experiment upon the subject nearest her heart, Mrs. Damerel had her little romance perfectly ready for Mr. Incledon when he came. "You must not blame me for a little disappointment to-day," she said, "though indeed I ought to have sent you word had I not been so busy. You must have seen that Rose was not herself yesterday. She has her father's fine organization, poor child, and all our troubles have told upon her. I have sent her to her old school, to Miss Margetts, whose care I can rely upon, for a little change. It will be handy in many ways, for I must go to town for shopping, and it will be less fatiguing to Rose to meet me there than to go up and down on the same day."

"Then she was not well yesterday?" said Mr. Incledon, over whose face various changes had passed of disappointment, annoyance, and relief.

"Could you not see that?" said the mother, smiling with gentle reproof. "When did Rose show temper before? She has her faults, but that is not one of them; but she has her father's fine organization. I don't hesitate to say now, when it is all over, that poverty brought us many annoyances and some privations, as it does to everybody, I suppose. Rose has borne up bravely, but of course she felt them; and it is a specialty with such highly-strung natures," said this elaborate deceiver, "that they never break down till the pressure is removed."

"Ah! I ought to have known it," said Mr. Incledon; "and, indeed," he added, after a pause, "what you say is a great relief, for I had begun to fear that so young a creature might have found out that she had been too hasty—that she did not know her own mind."

"It is not her mind, but her nerves and temperament," said the mother. "I shall leave her quite quiet for a few days."

"And must I leave her quiet too?"

"I think so, if you don't mind. I could not tell you at the time," said Mrs. Damerel, with absolute truth and candor such as gave the best possible effect when used as accompaniments to the pious fib, "for I knew you would have wished to help us, and I could not have allowed it; but there have been a great many things to put up with. You don't know what it is to be left to the tender mercies of a maid-of-all-work, and Rose has had to soil her poor little fingers, as I never thought to see a child of mine do; it is no disgrace, especially when it is all over," she added, with a little laugh.

"Disgrace! it is nothing but honor," said the lover, with some moisture starting into his eyes. He would have liked to kiss the poor little fingers of which her mother spoke with playful tenderness, and went away comparatively happy, wondering whether there was not something more to do than he had originally thought of by which he could show his pride and delight and loving homage to his Rose.

Poor Mrs. Damerel! I am afraid it was very wicked of her, as a clergywoman who ought to show a good example to the world in general; and she could have whipped Rose all the same for thus leaving her in the lurch; but still it was clever, and a gift which most women have to exercise, more or less.

But oh! the terrors which overwhelmed her soul when, after having dismissed Mr. Incledon, thus wrapped over again in a false security, she bethought herself that Rose had travelled to town in company with young Wodehouse; that they had been shut up for more than an hour together; that he had told his love-tale, and she had confided enough to him to leave him not hopeless, at least. Other things might be made to arrange themselves; but what was to be done with the always rebellious girl when the man she preferred—a young lover, impassioned and urgent—had come into the field?

CHAPTER XVI.

WHEN Rose found herself, after so strange and exciting a journey, within the tranquil shades of Miss Margetts' establishment for young ladies, it would be difficult to tell the strange hush which fell upon her. Almost before the door had closed upon Wodehouse, while still the rumble of the hansom in which he had brought her to her destination, and in which he now drove away, was in her ears, the hush, the chill, the tranquillity had begun to influence her. Miss Margetts, of course, was not up at half-past six on the summer morning, and it was an early housemaid, curious but drowsy, who admitted Rose, and took her, having some suspicion of so unusually early a visitor, with so little luggage, to the bare and forbidding apartment in which Miss Margetts generally received her "parents." The window looked out upon the little garden in front of the house, and the high wall which inclosed it; and there Rose seated herself to wait, all the energy and passion which had sustained, beginning to fail her, and dreary doubts of what her old school-mistress would say, and how she would receive her, filling her very soul. How strange is the stillness of the morning within such a populated house! nothing stirring but the faint, far-off noises in the kitchen—and she alone, with the big blank walls about her, feeling like a prisoner, as if she had been shut in to undergo some sentence. To be sure, in other circumstances this was just the moment which Rose would have chosen to be alone, and in which the recollection of the scene just ended, the words which she had heard, the looks that had been bent upon her, ought to have been enough to light up the dreariest place, and make her unconscious of external pallor and vacancy. But although the warmest sense of personal happiness which she had ever known in her life had come upon the girl all unawares ere she came here, yet the circumstances were so strange, and the complication of feeling so great, that all the light seemed to die out of the landscape when Edward left her. This very joy which had come to her so unexpectedly gave a different aspect to all the rest of her story. To fly from a marriage which was disagreeable to her, with no warmer wish than that of simply escaping from it, was one thing; but to fly with the aid of a lover, who made the flight an occasion of declaring himself, was another and very different matter. Her heart sank while she thought of the story she had to tell. Should she dare tell Miss Margetts about Edward? About Mr. Incledon it seemed now simple enough.

Miss Margetts was a kind woman, or one of her "young ladies" would not have thought of flying back to her for shelter in trouble; but she was always a little rigid and "particular," and when she heard Rose's story (with the careful exclusion of Edward) her mind was very much disturbed. She was sorry for the girl, but felt sure that her mother must be in the right, and trembled a little in the midst of her decorum, to consider what the world would think if she was found to receive girls who set themselves in opposition to their lawful guardians. "Was the gentleman not nice?" she asked, doubtfully; "was he very old? were his morals not what they ought to be? or has he any personal peculiarity which made him unpleasant? Except in the latter case, when indeed one must judge for one's self, I think you might have put full confidence in your excellent mother's judgment."

"Oh, it was not that; he is very good and nice," said Rose, confused and troubled. "It is not that I object to him; it is because I do not love him. How could I marry him when I don't care for him? But he is not a man to whom anybody could object."

"And he is rich, and fond of you, and not too old? I fear—I fear, my dear child, you have been very inconsiderate. You would soon have learned to love so good a man."

"Oh, Miss Anne," said Rose (for there were two sisters, and this was the youngest), "don't say so, please! I never could if I should live a hundred years."

"You will not live a hundred years; but you might have tried. Girls are pliable; or at least people think so; perhaps my particular position in respect to them makes me less sure of this than most people are. But still, that is the common idea. You would have learned to be fond of him if he were fond of you; unless, indeed"—

"Unless what?" cried Rose, intent upon suggestion of excuse.

"Unless," said Miss Margetts, solemnly, fixing her with the penetrating glance of an eye accustomed to command—"unless there is another gentleman in the case—unless you have allowed another image to enter your heart?"

Rose was unprepared for such an appeal. She answered it only by a scared look, and hid her face in her hands.

"Perhaps it will be best to have some breakfast," said Miss Margetts. "You must have been up very early to be here so soon; and I dare say you did not take anything before you started, not even a cup of tea?"

Rose had to avow this lack of common prudence, and try to eat docilely to please her protector; but the attempt was not very successful. A single night's watching is often enough to upset a youthful frame not accustomed to anything of the kind, and Rose was glad beyond description to be taken to one of the little white-curtained chambers which were so familiar to her, and left there to rest. How inconceivable it was that she should be there again! Her very familiarity with everything made the wonder greater. Had she never left that still, well-ordered place at all? or what strange current had drifted her back again? She lay down on the little white dimity bed, much too deeply affected with her strange position, she thought, to rest; but ere long had fallen fast asleep, poor child, with her hands clasped across her breast, and tears trembling upon her eyelashes. Miss Margetts, being a kind soul, was deeply touched when she looked into the room and found her so, and immediately went back to her private parlor and scored an adjective or two out of the letter she had written—a letter to Rose's mother, telling how startled she had been to find herself made unawares the confidant of the runaway, and begging Mrs. Damerel to believe that it was no fault of hers, though she assured her in the same breath that every attention should be paid to Rose's health and comfort. Mrs. Damerel would thus have been very soon relieved from her suspense, even if she had not received the despairing little epistle sent to her by Rose. Of Rose's note, however, her mother took no immediate notice. She wrote to Miss Margetts, thanking her, and assuring her that she was only too glad to think that her child was in such good hands. But she did not write to Rose. No one wrote to Rose; she was left for three whole days without a word, for even Wodehouse did not venture to send the glowing epistles which he wrote by the score, having an idea that an establishment for young ladies is a kind of Castle Dangerous, in which such letters as his would never be suffered to reach their proper owner, and might prejudice her with her jailers. These dreary days were dreary enough for all of them: for the mother, who was not so perfectly assured of being right in her mode of treatment as to be quite at ease on the subject; for the young lover, burning with impatience, and feeling every day to be a year; and for Rose herself, thus dropped into the stillness away from all that had excited and driven her desperate. To be delivered all at once out of even trouble which is of an exciting and stimulating character, and buried in absolute quiet, is a doubtful advantage in any case, at least to youth. Mr. Incledon bore the interval, not knowing all that was involved in it, with more calm than any of the others. He was quite amenable to Mrs. Damerel's advice not to disturb the girl with letters. After all, what was a week to a man secure of Rose's company for the rest of his life? He smiled a little at the refuge which her mother's care (he thought) had chosen for her—her former school! and wondered how his poor little Rose liked it; but otherwise was perfectly tranquil on the subject. As for poor young Wodehouse, he was to be seen about the railway station, every train that arrived from London, and haunted the precincts of the White House for news, and was as miserable as a young man in love and terrible uncertainty—with only ten days in which to satisfy himself about his future life and happiness—could be. What wild thoughts went through his mind as he answered "yes" and "no" to his mother's talk, and dutifully took walks with her, and called with her upon her friends, hearing Rose's approaching marriage everywhere talked of, and the "good luck" of the rector's family remarked upon! His heart was tormented by all these conversations, yet it was better to hear them, than to be out of the way of hearing altogether. Gretna Green, if Gretna Green should be feasible, was the only way he could think of, to get delivered from this terrible complication; and then it haunted him that Gretna Green had been "done away with," though he could not quite remember how. Ten days! and then the China seas for three long years; though Rose had not been able to conceal from him that he it was whom she loved, and not Mr. Incledon. Poor fellow! in his despair he thought of deserting, of throwing up his appointment and losing all his chances in life; and all these wild thoughts swayed upwards to a climax in the three days. He determined on the last of these that he would bear it no longer. He put a passionate letter in the post, and resolved to beard Mrs. Damerel in the morning and have it out.

More curious still, and scarcely less bewildering, was the strange trance of suspended existence in which Rose spent these three days. It was but two years since she had left Miss Margetts', and some of her friends were there still. She was glad to meet them, as much as she could be glad of anything in her preoccupied state, but felt the strangest difference—a difference which she was totally incapable of putting into words—between them and herself. Rose, without knowing it, had made a huge stride in life since she had left their bare school-room. I dare say her education might with much advantage have been carried on a great deal longer than it was, and that her power of thinking might have increased, and her mind been much improved, had she been sent to college afterwards, as boys are, and as some people think girls ought to be; but though she had not been to college, education of a totally different kind had been going on for Rose. She had made a step in life which carried her altogether beyond the placid region in which the other girls lived and worked. She was in the midst of problems which Euclid cannot touch, nor logic solve. She had to exercise choice in a matter concerning other lives as well as her own. She had to decide unaided between a true and a false moral duty, and to make up her mind which was true and which was false. She had to discriminate in what point Inclination ought to be considered a rule of conduct, and in what points it ought to be crushed as mere self-seeking; or whether it should not always be crushed, which was her mother's code; or if it ought to have supreme weight, which was her father's practice. This is not the kind of training which youth can get from schools, whether in Miss Margetts' establishment for young ladies, or even in learned Balliol. Rose, who had been subjected to it, felt, but could not tell why, as if she were years and worlds removed from the school and its duties. She could scarcely help smiling at the elder girls with their "deep" studies and their books, which were far more advanced intellectually than Rose. Oh, how easy the hardest grammar was, the difficulties of Goethe, or of Dante (or even of Thucydides or Perseus, but these she did not know), in comparison with this difficulty which tore her asunder! Even the moral and religious truths in which she had been trained from her cradle scarcely helped her. The question was one to be decided for herself and by herself, and by her for her alone.

And here is the question, dear reader, as the girl had to decide it. Self-denial is the rule of Christianity. It is the highest and noblest of duties when exercised for a true end. "Greater love hath no man than this, that a man lay down his life for his friend." Thus it has the highest sanction which any duty can have, and it is the very life and breath and essence of Christianity. This being the rule, is there one special case excepted in which you ought not to deny yourself? and is this case the individual one of Marriage? Allowing that in all other matters it is right to sacrifice your own wishes, where by doing so you benefit others, is it right to sacrifice your love and happiness in order to please your friends, and make a man happy who loves you, but whom you do not love? According to Mrs. Damerel this was so, and the sacrifice of a girl who made a loveless marriage for a good purpose was as noble as any other martyrdom for the benefit of country or family or race. Gentle reader, if you do not skip the statement of the question altogether, you will probably decide it summarily and wonder at Rose's indecision. But hers was no such easy way of dealing with the problem, which I agree with her in thinking is much harder than anything in Euclid. She was not by any means sure that this amount of self-sacrifice was not a duty. Her heart divined, her very intellect felt, without penetrating, a fallacy somewhere in the argument; but still the argument was very potent and not to be got over. She was not sure that to listen to Edward Wodehouse, and to suffer even an unguarded reply to drop from her lips, was not a sin. She was far from being sure that in any case it is safe or right to do what you like; and to do what you like in contradiction to your mother, to your engagement, to your plighted word—what could that be but a sin? She employed all her simple logic on the subject with little effect, for in strict logic she was bound over to marry Mr. Incledon, and now more than ever her heart resolved against marrying Mr. Incledon.

This question worked in her mind, presenting itself in every possible phase—now one side, now the other. And she dared not consult any one near, and none of those who were interested in its solution took any notice of her. She was left alone in unbroken stillness to judge for herself, to make her own conclusion. The first day she was still occupied with the novelty of her position—the fatigue and excitement of leaving home, and of all that had occurred since. The second day she was still strangely moved by the difference between herself and her old friends, and the sense of having passed beyond them into regions unknown to their philosophy, and from which she never could come back to the unbroken tranquillity of a girl's life. But on the third day the weight of her strange position weighed her down utterly. She watched the distribution of the letters with eyes growing twice their natural size, and a pang indescribable at her heart. Did they mean to leave her alone then? to take no further trouble about her? to let her do as she liked, that melancholy privilege which is prized only by those who do not possess it? Had Edward forgotten her, though he had said so much two days ago? had her mother cast her off, despising her, as a rebel? Even Mr. Incledon, was he going to let her be lost to him without an effort? Rose had fled hoping (she believed) for nothing so much as to lose herself and be heard of no more; but oh! the heaviness which drooped over her very soul when for three days she was let alone! Wonder, consternation, indignation, arose one after another in her heart. They had all abandoned her. The lover whom she loved, and the lover whom she did not love, alike. What was love then? a mere fable, a thing which perished when the object of it was out of sight? When she had time to think, indeed, she found this theory untenable, for had not Edward been faithful to her at the other end of the world? and yet what did he mean now?

On the third night Rose threw herself on her bed in despair, and sobbed till midnight. Then a mighty resolution arose in her mind. She would relieve herself of the burden. She would go to the fountain-head, to Mr. Incledon himself, and lay the whole long tale before him. He was good, he was just, he had always been kind to her; she would abide by what he said. If he insisted that she should marry him, she must do so; better that than to be thrown off by everybody, to be left for days or perhaps for years alone in Miss Margetts'. And if he were generous, and decided otherwise! In that case neither Mrs. Damerel nor any one else could have anything to say—she would put it into his hands.

She had her hat on when she came down to breakfast next morning, and her face, though pale, had a little resolution in it, better than the despondency of the first three days. "I am going home," she said, as the school-mistress looked at her, surprised.

"It is the very best thing you can do, my dear," said Miss Margetts, giving her a more cordial kiss than usual. "I did not like to advise it; but it is the very best thing you can do."

Rose took her breakfast meekly, not so much comforted as Miss Margetts had intended by this approval. Somehow she felt as if it must be against her own interest since Miss Margetts approved of it, and she was in twenty minds then not to go. When the letters came in she said to herself that there could be none for her, and went and stood at the window, turning her back that she might not see; and it was while she was standing thus, pretending to gaze out upon the high wall covered with ivy, that, in the usual contradiction of human affairs, Edward Wodehouse's impassioned letter was put into her hands. There she read how he too had made up his mind not to bear it longer; how he was going to her mother to have an explanation with her. Should she wait for the result of this explanation, or should she carry out her own determination and go?

"Come, Rose, I will see you safely to the station: there is a cab at the door," said Miss Margetts.

Rose turned round, her eyes dewy and moist with those tears of love and consolation which refresh and do not scorch as they come. She looked up timidly to see whether she might ask leave to stay; but the cab was waiting, and Miss Margetts was ready, and her own hat on and intention declared; she was ashamed to turn back when she had gone so far. She said good-by accordingly to the elder sister, and meekly followed Miss Anne into the cab. Had it been worth while winding herself up to the resolution of flight for so little? Was her first experiment of resistance really over, and the rebel going home, with arms grounded and banners trailing? It was ignominious beyond all expression—but what was she to do?

"My dear," said Miss Margetts, in the cab, which jolted very much, and now and then took away her breath, "I hope you are going with your mind in a better frame, and disposed to pay attention to what your good mother says. *She* must know best. Try and remember this, whatever happens. You ought to say it to yourself all the way down as a penance, 'My mother knows best.'"

"But how can she know best what I am feeling?" said Rose. "It must be myself who must judge of that."

"You may be sure she knows a great deal more, and has given more thought to it than you suppose," said the school-mistress; "dear child, make me happy by promising that you will follow her advice."

Rose made no promise, but her heart sank as she thus set out upon her return journey. It was less terrible when she found herself alone in the railway carriage, and yet it was more terrible as she realized what desperation had driven her to. She was going back as she went away, with no question decided, no resolution come to, with only new complications to encounter, without the expedient of flight, which could not be repeated. Ought she not to have been more patient, to have tried to put up with silence? That could not have lasted forever. But now she was going to put herself back in the very heart of the danger, with no ground gained, but something lost. Well! she said to herself, at least it would be over. She would know the worst, and there would be no further appeal against it. If happiness was over too, she would have nothing to do in all the life before her—nothing to do but to mourn over the loss of it, and teach herself to do without it; and suspense would be over. She got out of the carriage, pulling her veil over her face, and took an unfrequented path which led away across the fields to the road near Whitton, quite out of reach of the Green and all its inhabitants. It was a long walk, but the air and the movement did her good. She went on swiftly and quietly, her whole mind bent upon the interview she was going to seek. All beyond was a blank to her. This one thing, evident and definite, seemed to fix and to clear her dazzled eyesight. She met one or two acquaintances, but they did not recognize her through her veil, though she saw them, and recollected them ever after, as having had something to do with that climax and agony of her youth; and thus Rose reached Whitton, with its soft, abundant summer woods, and, her heart beating louder and louder, hastened her steps as she drew near her destination, almost running across the park to Mr. Incledon's door.

CHAPTER XVII.

"Rose! is it possible?" he cried. She was standing in the midst of that great, luxurious, beautiful drawing-room, of which he hoped she was to be the queen and mistress, her black dress breaking harshly upon all the soft harmony of neutral tints around. Her face, which he saw in the glass as he entered the room, was framed in the large veil which she had thrown back over her hat, and which drooped down on her shoulders on either side. She was quite pale—her cheeks blanched out of all trace of color, with something of that chilled and spiritual light which sometimes appears in the colorless clearness of the sky after a storm. Her eyes were larger than usual, and had a dilated, exhausted look. Her face was full of a speechless, silent eagerness—eagerness which could wait, yet was almost beyond the common artifices of concealment. Her hands were softly clasped together, with a certain eloquence in their close pressure, supporting each other. All this Mr. Incledon saw in the glass before he could see her; and, though he went in with lively and joyful animation, the sight startled him a little. He came forward, however, quite cheerfully, though his heart failed him, and took the clasped hands into his own.

"I did not look for such a bright interruption to a dull morning," he said; "but what a double pleasure it is to see you here! How good of you to come to bring me the happy news of your return!"

"Mr. Incledon," she said hastily, "oh! do not be glad—don't say I am good. I have come to you first without seeing mamma. I have come to say a great deal—a very great deal—to you; and to ask—your advice—and if you will tell me—what to do."

Her voice sank quite low before these final words were said.

"My darling," he said, "you are very serious and solemn. What can you want advice about? But whatever it is, you have a right to the very best I can give you. Let me hear what the difficulty is. Here is a chair for you—one of your own choice, the new ones. Tell me if you think it comfortable; and then tell me what this terrible difficulty is."

"Oh, don't take it so lightly," said Rose, "please don't. I am very, very unhappy, and I have determined to tell everything and to let you judge me. You have the best right."

"Thanks for saying so," he said, with a smile, kissing her hand. He thought she meant that as she was so surely his, it was naturally his part to think for her and help her in everything. What so natural? And then he awaited her disclosure, still smiling, expecting some innocent dilemma, such as would be in keeping with her innocent looks. He could not understand her, nor the gravity of the appeal to him which she had come to make.

"Oh, Mr. Incledon!" cried Rose, "if you knew what I meant, you would not smile—you would not take it so easily. I have come to tell you everything—how I have lied to you and been a cheat and a deceiver. Oh! don't laugh! you don't know—you don't know how serious it is!"

"Nay, dear child," he said, "do you want to frighten me? for if you do, you must think of something more likely than that you are a cheat and deceiver. Come now, I will be serious—as serious as a judge. Tell me what it is, Rose."

"It is about you and me," she said suddenly, after a little pause.

"Ah!"—this startled him for the first time. His grasp tightened upon her hand; but he used no more endearing words. "Go on," he said, softly.

"May I begin at the beginning? I should like to tell you everything. When you first spoke to me, Mr. Incledon, I told you there was some one"—

"Ah!" cried Mr. Incledon again, still more sharply, "he is here now. You have seen him since he came back?"

"It is not that," said Rose. "Oh! let me tell you from the beginning. I said then that he had never said anything to me. I could not tell you his name because I did not know what his feelings were—only my own, of which I was ashamed. Mr. Incledon, have patience with me a little. Just before he went away he came to the rectory to say good-by. He sent up a message to ask me to come down, but mamma went down instead. Then his mother sent me a little note, begging me to go to bid him good-by. It was while papa was ill; he held my hand, and would not let me. I begged him, only for a minute; but he held my hand and would not let me go. I had to sit there and listen, and hear the door open and shut, and then steps in the hall and on the gravel, and then mamma coming slowly back again, as if nothing had happened, up-stairs and along the corridor. Oh! I thought she was walking on my heart!"

Rose's eyes were so full that she did not see how her listener looked. He held her hand still, but with his disengaged hand he partially covered his face.

"Then after that," she resumed, pausing for breath, "all our trouble came. I did not seem to care for anything. It is dreadful to say it—and I never did say it till now—but I don't think I felt so unhappy as I ought about poor papa; I was so unhappy before. It did not break my heart as grief ought to do. I was only dull—dull—miserable, and did not care for anything; but then everybody was unhappy; and there was good reason for it, and no one thought of me. It went on like that till you came."

Here he stirred a little and grasped her hand more tightly. What she had said hitherto had not been pleasant to him; but yet it was all before he had made his appearance as her suitor—all innocent, visionary—the very romance of youthful liking. Such an early dream of the dawning any man, even the most rigid, might forgive to his bride.

"You came—oh! Mr. Incledon, do not be angry—I want to tell you everything. If it vexes you and hurts you, will you mind? You came; and mamma told me that same night. Oh, how frightened I was and miserable! Everything seemed to turn round with me. She said you loved me, and that you were very good and very kind,—but that I knew,—and would do so much for the boys, and be a comfort and help to her in our great poverty." At these words he stirred again and loosened, but did not quite let go, his grasp of her hand. Rose was, without knowing it, acting like a skilful surgeon, cutting deep and sharp, that the pain might be over the sooner. He leaned his head on his other hand, turning it away from her, and from time to time stirred unconsciously when the sting was too much for him, but did not speak. "And she said more than this. Oh, Mr. Incledon! I must tell you everything, as if you were my own heart. She told me that papa had not been—considerate for us, as he should have been; that he liked his own way and his own pleasure best; and that I was following him—that I was doing the same—ruining the boys' prospects and prolonging our great poverty, because I did not want to marry you, though you had promised to help them and set everything right."

Mr. Incledon dropped Rose's hand; he turned half away from her, supporting his head upon both of his hands, so that she did not see his face. She did not know how cruel she was, nor did she mean to be cruel, but simply historical, telling him everything, as if she had been speaking to her own heart.

"Then I saw you," said Rose, "and told you—or else I thought I told you—and you did not mind, but would not, though I begged you, give up. And everything went on for a long, long time. Sometimes I was very wretched; sometimes my heart felt quite dull, and I did not seem to mind what happened. Sometimes I forgot for a little while—and oh! Mr. Incledon, now and then, though I tried very hard, I could not help thinking of—him. I never did when I could help it; but sometimes when I saw the lights on Ankermead, or remembered something he had said—And all this time mamma would talk to me of people who prefer their own will to the happiness of others; of all the distress and misery it brought when we indulged ourselves and our whims and fancies; of how much better it was to do what was right than what we liked. My head got confused sometimes, and I felt as if she was wrong, but I could not put it into words; for how could it be right to deceive a good man like you—to let you give your love for nothing, and marry you without caring for you? But I am not clever enough to argue with mamma. Once, I think, for a minute, I got the better of her; but when she told me that I was preferring my own will to everybody's happiness, it went to my heart, and what could I say? Do you remember the day when it was all settled at last and made up?"

This was more than the poor man could bear. He put up one hand with a wild gesture to stop her, and uttered a hoarse exclamation; but Rose was too much absorbed in her story to stop.

"The night before I had gone down into the rectory garden, where he and I used to talk, and there I said good-by to him in my heart, and made a kind of grave over him, and gave him up for ever and ever—oh! don't you know how?" said Rose, the tears dropping on her black dress. "Then I was willing that it should be settled how you pleased; and I never, never allowed myself to think of him any more. When he came into my head, I went to the school-room, or I took a hard bit of music, or I talked to mamma, or heard Patty her lessons. I would not, because I thought it would be wicked to you, and you so good to me, Mr. Incledon. Oh! if you had only been my brother, or my—cousin (she had almost said, father or uncle, but by good luck forbore), how fond I should have been of you!—and I am fond of you," said Rose, softly, proffering the hand which he had put away, and laying it gently upon his arm.

He shook his head, and made a little gesture as if to put it off, but yet the touch and the words went to his heart.

"Now comes the worst of all," said Rose. "I know it will hurt you, and yet I must tell you. After that there came the news of uncle Ernest's death; and that he had left his money to us, and that we were well off again—better than we had ever been. Oh, forgive me! forgive me!" she said, clasping his arm with both her hands, "when I heard it, it seemed to me all in a moment that I was free. Mamma said that all the sacrifices we had been making would be unnecessary henceforward; what she meant was the things we had been doing—dusting the rooms, putting the table straight, helping in the house—oh! as if these could be called sacrifices! But I thought she meant me. You are angry—you are angry!" said Rose. "I could not expect anything else. But it was not you, Mr. Incledon; it was that I hated to be married. I could not—could not make up my mind to it. I turned into a different creature when I thought that I was free."

The simplicity of the story disarmed the man, sharp and bitter as was the sting and mortification of listening to this too artless tale. "Poor child!

poor child!" he murmured, in a softer tone, unclasping the delicate fingers from his arm; and then, with an effort, "I am not angry. Go on; let me hear it to the end."

"When mamma saw how glad I was, she stopped it all at once," said Rose, controlling herself. "She said I was just the same as ever—always self-indulgent, thinking of myself, not of others—and that I was as much bound as ever by honor. There was no longer any question of the boys, or of help to the family; but she said honor was just as much to be considered, and that I had pledged my word"—

"Rose," quietly said Mr. Incledon, "spare me what you can of these discussions—you had pledged your word?"

She drew away half frightened, not expecting the harsher tone in his voice, though she had expected him to "be angry," as she said. "Forgive me," she went on, subdued, "I was so disappointed that it made me wild. I did not know what to do. I could not see any reason for it now—any good in it; and, at last, when I was almost crazy with thinking, I—ran away."

"You ran away?"—Mr. Incledon raised his head, indignant. "Your mother has lied all round," he said, fiercely; then, bethinking himself, "I beg your pardon. Mrs. Damerel no doubt had her reasons for what she said."

"There was only one place I could go to," said Rose, timidly, "Miss Margetts', where I was at school. I went up to the station for the early train that nobody might see me. I was very much frightened. Some one was standing there; I did not know who he was—he came by the train, I think; but after I had got into the carriage he came in after me. Mr. Incledon! it was not his fault, neither his nor mine. I had not been thinking of him. It was not for him, but only not to be married—to be free"—

"Of me," he said, with a bitter smile; "but in short, you met, whether by intention or not—and Mr. Wodehouse took advantage of his opportunities?"

"He told me," said Rose, not looking at Mr. Incledon, "what I had known ever so long without being told; but I said nothing to him; what could I say? I told him all that had happened. He took me to Miss Margetts', and there we parted," said Rose, with a momentary pause and a deep sigh.

"Since then I have done nothing but think and think. No one has come near me—no one has written to me. I have been left alone to go over and over it all in my own mind. I have done so till I was nearly mad, or at least, everything seemed going round with me and everything confused, and I could not tell what was right and what was wrong. Oh!" cried Rose, lifting her head in natural eloquence, with eyes which looked beyond him, and a certain elevation and abstraction in her face, "I don't think it is a thing in which only right and wrong are to be considered. When you love one and do not love another, it must mean something; and to marry unwillingly, that is nothing to content a man. It is a wrong to him; it is not doing right; it is treating him unkindly, cruelly! It is as if he wanted you, anyhow, like a cat or a dog; not as if he wanted you worthily, as his companion." Rose's courage failed her after this little outburst; her high looks came down, her voice sank and faltered, her head drooped. She rose up, and clasping her hands together, went on in low tones: "Mr. Incledon, I am engaged to you; I belong to you. I trust your justice and your kindness more than anything else. If you say I am to marry you, I will do it. Take it now into your own hands. If I think of it any more I will go mad; but I will do whatever you say."

He was walking up and down the room, with his face averted, and with pain and anger and humiliation in his heart. All this time he had believed he was leading Rose towards the reasonable love for him which was all he hoped for. He had supposed himself in almost a lofty position, offering to this young, fresh, simple creature more in every way than she could ever have had but for him—a higher position, a love more noble than any foolish boy-and-girl attachment. To find out in a moment how very different the real state of the case had been, and to have conjured up before him the picture of a martyr-girl, weeping and struggling, and a mother "with a host of petty maxims preaching down her daughter's heart," was intolerable to him. He had never been so mortified, so humbled in all his life. He walked up and down the room in a ferment, with that sense of the unbearable which is so bitter. Unbearable!—yet to be borne somehow; a something not to be ignored or cast off. It said much for Rose's concluding appeal that he heard it at all, and took in the meaning of it in his agitation and hot, indignant rage; but he did hear it, and it touched him. "If you say I am to marry you, I will do it." He stopped short in his impatient walk. Should he say it—in mingled despite and love—and keep her to her word? He came up to her and took her clasped hands within his, half in anger, half in tenderness, and looked her in the face.

"If I say you are to marry me, you will do it? You pledge yourself to that? You will marry me if I please?"

"Yes," said Rose, very pale, looking up at him steadfastly. She neither trembled nor hesitated. She had gone beyond any superficial emotion.

Then he stooped and kissed her with a passion which was rough—almost brutal. Rose's pale face flushed, and her slight figure wavered like a reed; but she neither shrank nor complained. He had a right to dictate to her—she had put it into his hands. The look of those large, innocent eyes, from which all conflict had departed, which had grown abstract in their wistfulness, holding fast at least by one clear duty, went to his heart. He kept looking at her, but she did not quail. She had no thought but her word, and to do what she had said.

"Rose," he said, "you are a cheat, like all women. You come to me with this face, and insult me and stab me, and say then you will do what I tell you, and stand there, looking at me with innocent eyes like an angel. How could you find it in your heart—if you have a heart—to tell me all this? How dare you put that dainty little cruel foot of yours upon my neck, and scorn and torture me—how dare you, how dare you!" There came a glimmer into his eyes, as if it might have been some moisture forced up by means beyond his control, and he held her hands with such force that it seemed to Rose he shook her, whether willingly or not. But she did not shrink. She looked up at him, her eyes growing more and more wistful, and though he hurt her, did not complain.

"It was that you might know all the truth," she said, almost under her breath. "Now you know everything and can judge—and I will do as you say."

He held her so for a minute longer, which seemed eternity to Rose; then he let her hands drop, and turned away.

"It is not you who are to blame," he said, "not you, but your mother, who would have sold you. Good God! do all women traffic in their own flesh and blood?"

"Do not say so!" cried Rose, with sudden tears; "you shall not! I will not hear it! She has been wrong; but that was not what she meant."

Mr. Incledon laughed—his mood seemed to have changed all in a moment. "Come Rose," he said, "perhaps it is not quite decorous for you, a young lady, to be here alone. Come! I will take you to your mother, and then you shall hear what I have got to say."

She walked out of the great house by his side as if she were in a dream. What did he mean? The suspense became terrible to her; for she could not guess what he would say. Her poor little feet twisted over each other and she stumbled and staggered with weakness as she went along beside him—stumbled so much that he made her take his arm, and led her carefully along, with now and then a kind but meaningless word. Before they entered the White House, Rose was leaning almost her whole weight upon his supporting arm. The world was swimming and floating around, the trees going in circles, now above, now below her, she thought. She was but half conscious when she went in, stumbling across the threshold, to the little hall, all bright with Mr. Incledon's flowers. Was she to be his, too, like one of them—a flower to carry about wherever he went, passive and helpless as one of the plants—past resistance, almost past suffering? "I am afraid she is ill; take care of her, Agatha," said Mr. Incledon to her sister, who came rushing open-mouthed and open-eyed; and, leaving her there, he strode unannounced into the drawing-room to meet the real author of his discomfiture, an antagonist more worthy of his steel and against whom he could use his weapons with less compunction than against the submissive Rose.

Mrs. Damerel had been occupied all the morning with Mr. Nolan, who had obeyed her summons on the first day of Rose's flight, but whom she had dismissed when she ascertained where her daughter was, assuring him that to do nothing was the best policy, as indeed it had proved to be. The curate had gone home that evening obedient; but moved by the electrical impulse which seemed to have set all minds interested in Rose in motion on that special day, had come back this morning to urge her mother to go to her or to allow him to go to her. Mr. Nolan's presence had furnished an excuse to Mrs. Damerel for declining to receive poor young Wodehouse, who had asked to see her immediately after breakfast. She was discussing even then with the curate how to get rid of him, what to say to him, and what it was best to do to bring Rose back to her duty. "I can't see so clear as you that it's her duty, in all the circumstances," the curate had said doubtfully. "What have circumstances to do with a matter of right and wrong—of truth and honor?" cried Mrs. Damerel. "She must keep her word." It was at this precise moment of the conversation that Mr. Incledon appeared; and I suppose she must have seen something in his aspect and the expression of his face that showed some strange event had happened. Mrs. Damerel gave a low cry, and the muscles of Mr. Incledon's mouth were moved by one of those strange contortions which in such cases are supposed to do duty for a smile. He bowed low, with a mock reverence, to Mr. Nolan, but did not put out his hand.

"I presume," he said, "that this gentleman is in the secret of my humiliation, as well as the rest of the family, and that I need not hesitate to say what I have to say before him. It is pleasant to think that so large a circle of friends interest themselves in my affairs."

"What do you mean?" said Mrs. Damerel. "Your humiliation! Have you sustained any humiliation? I do not know what you mean."

"Oh! I can make it very clear," he said, with the same smile. "Your daughter has been with me; I have just brought her home."

"What! Rose?" said Mrs. Damerel, starting to her feet; but he stopped her before she could make a step.

"Do not go," he said; "It is more important that you should stay here. What have I done to you that you should have thus humbled me to the dust? Did I ask you to sell her to me? Did I want a wife for hire? Should I have authorized any one to persecute an innocent girl, and drive her almost mad for me? Good heavens, for me! Think of it, if you can. Am I the sort of man to be forced on a girl—to be married as a matter of duty? How dared you—how dared any one insult me so!"

Mrs. Damerel, who had risen to her feet, sank into a chair, and covered her face with her hands. I do not think she had ever once taken into consideration this side of the question.

"Mr. Incledon," she stammered, "you have been misinformed; you are mistaken. Indeed, indeed, it is; not so."

"Misinformed!" he cried; "mistaken! I have my information from the very fountain-head—from the poor child who has been all but sacrificed to this supposed commercial transaction between you and me, which I disown altogether for my part. I never made such a bargain, nor thought of it. I never asked to buy your Rose. I might have won her, perhaps," he added, calming himself with an effort, "if you had let us alone, or I should have discovered at once that it was labor lost. Look here. We have been friends, and I never thought of you till to-day but with respect and kindness. How could you put such an affront on me?"

"Gently, gently," said Mr. Nolan, growing red; "you go too far, sir. If Mrs. Damerel has done wrong, it was a mistake of the judgment, not of the heart."

"The heart!" he cried, contemptuously; "how much heart was there in it? On poor Rose's side, a broken one; on mine, a heart deceived and deluded. Pah! do not speak to me of hearts or mistakes; I am too deeply mortified—too much wronged for that."

"Mr. Incledon," said Mrs. Damerel, rising, pale yet self-possessed, "I may have done wrong, as you say; but what I have done, I did for my child's advantage and for yours. You were told she did not love you, but you persevered; and I believed, and believe still, that when she knew you better—when she was your wife—she would love you. I may have pressed her too far; but it was no more a commercial transaction—no more a sale of my daughter"—she said, with a burning flush coming over her face—"no more than I tell you. You do me as much wrong as you say I have done you—Rose! Rose!"

Rose came in followed by Agatha, with her hat off, which showed more clearly the waste which emotion and fatigue, weary anxiety, waiting, abstinence, and mental suffering had worked upon her face. She had her hands clasped loosely yet firmly, in the attitude which had become habitual to her, and a pale smile like the wannest of winter sunshine on her face. She came up very quietly, and stood between the two like a ghost. Agatha said, who stood trembling behind her.

"Mamma, do not be angry," she said, softly; "I have told him everything, and I am quite ready to do whatever he decides. In any case, he ought to know everything, for it is he who is most concerned—he and I."

CHAPTER XVIII.

CAPTAIN WODEHOUSE did not get admission to the White House that day until the afternoon. He was not to be discouraged, though the messages he got were of a depressing nature enough. "Mrs. Damerel was engaged, and could not see him; would he come later?" "Mrs. Damerel was still engaged—more engaged than ever."

And while Mary Jane held the door ajar, Edward heard a voice raised high, with an indignant tone, speaking continuously, which was the voice of Mr. Incledon, though he did not identify it. Later still, Mrs. Damerel was still engaged; but, as he turned despairing from the door, Agatha rushed out, with excited looks, and with a message that if he came back at three o'clock her mother would see him.

"Rose has come home, and oh! there has been such a business!" Agatha whispered into his ear before she rushed back again. She knew a lover, and especially a favored lover, by instinct, as some girls do; but Agatha had the advantage of always knowing her own mind, and never would be the centre of any imbroglio, like the unfortunate Rose.

"Are you going back to the White House again?" said Mrs. Wodehouse. "I wonder how you can be so servile, Edward. I would not go, hat in hand, to any girl, if I were you; and when you know that she is engaged to another man, and he a great deal better off than you are! How can you show so little spirit? There are more Roses in the garden than one, and sweeter Roses, and richer, would be glad to have you. If I had thought you had so little proper pride, I should never have wished you to come here."

"I don't think I have any proper pride," said Edward, trying to make a feeble joke of it; "I have to come home now and then to know what it means."

"You were not always so poor-spirited," said his mother; "it is that silly girl who has turned your head. And she is not even there; she has gone up to town to get her trousseau and choose her wedding silks, so they say; and you may be sure, if she is engaged like that, she does not want to be reminded of you."

"I suppose not," said Edward, drearily; "but as I promised to go back, I think I must. I ought at least to bid them good-by."

"Oh! if that is all," said Mrs. Wodehouse, pacified, "go, my dear; and mind you put the very best face upon it. Don't look as if it were anything to you; congratulate them, and say you are glad to hear that any one so nice as Mr. Incledon is to be the gentleman. Oh! if I were in your place, I should know what to say! I should give Miss Rose something to remember. I should tell her I hoped she would be happy in her grand house, and was glad to hear that the settlements were everything they ought to be. She would feel that, you may be sure; for a girl that sets up for romance and poetry and all that don't like to be supposed mercenary. She should not soon forget her parting with me."

"Do you think I wish to hurt and wound her?" said Edward. "Surely not. If she is happy, I will wish her more happiness. She has never harmed me—no, mother. It cannot do a man any harm, even if it makes him unhappy, to think of a woman as I think of Rose."

"Oh! you have no spirit," cried Mrs. Wodehouse; "I don't know how a son of mine can take it so easily. Rose, indeed! Her very name makes my blood boil!"

But Edward's blood was very far from boiling as he walked across the Green for the third time that day. The current of life ran cold and low in him. The fiery determination of the morning to "have it out" with Mrs. Damerel, and know his fate and Rose's fate, had fallen into a despairing resolution at least to see her for the last time, to bid her forget everything that had passed, and try himself to forget. If her fate was sealed, and no longer in her own power to alter, that was all a generous man could do; and he felt sure, from the voices he had heard, and from the air of agitation about the house, and from Agatha's hasty communication, that this day had been a crisis to more than himself. He met Mr. Incledon as he approached the house. His rival looked at him gravely without a smile, and passed him with an abrupt "good morning." Mr. Incledon had not the air of a triumphant lover, and there was something of impatience and partial offence in his look as his eyes lingered for a moment upon the young sailor; so it appeared to Edward, though I think it was rather regret, and a certain wistful envy that was in Mr. Incledon's eyes. This young fellow, not half so clever, or so cultivated, or so important as himself, had won the prize which he had tried for and failed. The baffled man was still disturbed by unusual emotion, but he was not ungenerous in his sentiments; but then the other believed that he himself was the failure, and that Mr. Incledon had succeeded, and interpreted his looks, as we all do, according to the commentary in our own minds. Edward went on more depressed than ever after this meeting. Just outside the White House he encountered Mr. Nolan, going out to walk with the children. "Now that the gale is over, the little boats are going out for a row," said the curate, looking at him with a smile. It was not like Mr. Nolan's usual good nature, poor Edward thought. He was ushered in at once to the drawing-room, where Mrs. Damerel sat in a great chair, leaning back, with a look of weakness and exhaustion quite out of keeping with her usual energy. She held out her hand to him without rising. Her eyes were red, as if she had been shedding tears, and there was a flush upon her face. Altogether, her appearance bewildered him; no one in the world had ever seen Mrs. Damerel looking like this before.

"I am afraid you will think me importunate, coming back so often," he said, "but I felt that I must see you. Not that I come with much hope; but still it is better to know the very worst, if there is no good to hear."

"It depends on what you think worst or best," she said. "Mr. Wodehouse, you told me you were promoted—are captain now, and you have a ship?"

"Commander: and alas! under orders for China, with ten days' more leave," he said, with a faint smile; "though perhaps, on the whole, that may be best. Mrs. Damerel, may I not ask—for Rose? Pardon me for calling her so—I can't think of her otherwise. If it is all settled and made up, and my poor chance over, may I not see her, only for a few minutes? If you think what a dismal little story mine has been—sent away without seeing her a year ago, then raised into sudden hope by our chance meeting the other morning, and now, I suppose, sentenced to banishment forever"—

"Stay a little," she said; "I have had a very exciting day, and I am much worn out. Must you go in ten days?"

"Alas!" said Wodehouse, "and even my poor fortnight got with such difficulty—though perhaps on the whole it is better, Mrs. Damerel."

"Yes," she said, "have patience a moment; things have turned out very differently from what I wished. I cannot pretend to be pleased, scarcely resigned to what you have all done between you. You have nothing to offer my daughter, nothing! and she has nothing to contribute on her side. It is all selfish inclination, what you liked, not what was best, that has swayed you. You had not self-denial enough to keep silent; she had not self-denial enough to consider that this is not a thing for a day but for life; and the consequences, I suppose, as usual, will fall upon me. All my life I have had nothing to do but toil to make up for the misfortunes caused by self-indulgence. Others have had their will and pleasure, and I have paid the penalty. I thought for once it might have been different, but I have been mistaken, as you see."

"You forget that I have no clue to your meaning—that you are speaking riddles," said Wodehouse, whose depressed heart had begun to rise and flutter and thump against his young breast.

"Ah; that is true," said Mrs. Damerel, rising with a sigh. "Well, I wash my hands of it; and for the rest you will prefer to hear it from Rose rather than from me."

He stood in the middle of the room speechless when she closed the door behind her, and heard her soft steps going in regular measure through the still house, as Rose had heard them once. How still it was! the leaves fluttering at the open window, the birds singing, Mrs. Damerel's footsteps sounding fainter, his heart beating louder. But he had not very long to wait.

Mr. Nolan and the children went out on the river, and rowed up that long, lovely reach past Alfredsbury, skirting the bank, which was pink with branches of the wild rose and sweet with the feathery flowers of the Queen of the Meadows. Dick flattered himself that he pulled an excellent bow, and the curate, who loved the children's chatter, and themselves, humored the boy to the top of his bent. Agatha steered, and felt it an important duty, and Patty, who had nothing else to do, leaned her weight over the side of the boat, and did her best to capsize it, clutching at the wild roses and the meadow-queen. They shipped their oars and floated down with the stream when they had gone as far as they cared to go, and went up the hill again to the White House in a perfect bower of wild flowers, though the delicate rose blossoms began to droop in the warm grasp of the children before they got home. When they rushed in, flooding the house all through and through with their voices and their joyous breath and their flowers, they found all the rooms empty, the drawing-room silent, in a green repose, and not a creature visible. But while Agatha rushed up-stairs, calling upon her mother and Rose, Mr. Nolan saw a sight from the window which set his mind at rest. Two young figures together, one leaning on the other—two heads bent close, talking too low for any hearing but their own. The curate looked at them with a smile and a sigh. They had attained the height of blessedness. What better could the world give them? and yet the good curate's sigh was not all for the disappointed, nor his smile for their happiness alone.

The lovers were happy; but there are drawbacks to every mortal felicity. The fact that Edward had but nine days left, and that their fate must after that be left in obscurity, was, as may be supposed, a very serious drawback to their happiness. But their good fortune did not forsake them; or rather, to speak more truly, the disappointed lover did not forsake the girl who had appealed to him, who had mortified and tortured him, and promised with all the unconscious cruelty of candor to marry him if he told her to do so. Mr. Incledon went straight to town from the White House, intent on finishing the work he had begun. He had imposed on Mrs. Damerel as a duty to him, as a recompense for all that he had suffered at her hands, the task of receiving Wodehouse, and sanctioning the love which her daughter had given; and he went up to town to the Admiralty, to his friend whose unfortunate leniency had permitted the young sailor to return home. Mr. Incledon treated the matter lightly, making a joke of it. "I told you he was not to come home, but to be sent off as far as possible," he said.

"Why, what harm could the poor young fellow do in a fortnight?" said my lord. "I find I knew his father—a fine fellow and a good officer. The son shall be kept in mind, both for his sake and yours."

"He has done all the harm that was apprehended in his fortnight," said Mr. Incledon, "and now you must give him an extension of leave—enough to be married in. There's nothing else for it. You ought to do your best for him, for it is your fault."

Upon which my lord, who was of a genial nature, laughed and inquired into the story, which Mr. Incledon related to him after a fashion, in a way which, amused him hugely. The consequence was that Commander Wodehouse got his leave extended to three months, and was transferred from the China station to the Mediterranean. Mr. Incledon never told them who was the author of this benefit, though I think they had little difficulty in guessing. He sent Rose a *parure* of pearls and turquoises, simple enough for her youth and the position she had preferred to his, and sent the diamonds which had been reset for her back to his bankers; and then he went abroad. He did not go back to Whitton, even for necessary arrangements, but sent for all he wanted; and after that morning's work in the White House, returned to Dinglefield no more for years.

After this there was no possible reason for delay, and Rose was married to her sailor in the parish church by good Mr. Nolan, and instead of any other wedding tour went off to cruise with him in the Mediterranean. She had regained her bloom, and merited her old name again before the day of the simple wedding. Happiness brought back color and fragrance to the Rose in June; but traces of the storm that had almost crushed her never altogether disappeared, from her heart at least, if they did from her face. She cried over Mr. Incledon's letter the day before she became Edward Wodehouse's wife. She kissed the turquoises when she fastened them about her pretty neck. Love is the best, no doubt; but it would be hard if to other sentiments, less intense, even a bride might not spare a tear.

As for the mothers on either side, they were both indifferently satisfied. Mrs. Wodehouse would not unbend so much for months after as to say anything but "Good morning" to Mrs. Damerel, who had done her best to make her boy unhappy; and as for the marriage, now that it was accomplished after so much fuss and bother, it was after all nothing of a match for Edward. Mrs. Damerel, on her side, was a great deal too proud to offer any explanations except such as were absolutely necessary to those few influential friends who must be taken into every one's confidence who desires to keep a place in society. She told those confidants frankly enough that Edward and Rose had met accidentally, and that a youthful love, supposed to be over long ago, had burst forth again so warmly that nothing could be done but to tell Mr. Incledon; and that he had behaved like a hero. The Green for a little while was very angry at Rose; the ladies shook their heads at her, and said how very, very hard it was on poor Mr. Incledon. But Mr. Incledon was gone, and Whitton shut up, while Rose still remained with all the excitement of a pretty wedding in prospect, and "a perfect romance" in the shape of a love-story. Gradually, therefore, the girl was forgiven; the richer neighbors went up to town and bought their presents, the poorer ones looked over their stores to see what they could give, and the girls made pieces of lace for her, and pin-cushions, and antimacassars; and thus her offence was condoned by all the world. Though Mrs. Damerel asked but a few people to the breakfast, the church was crowded to see the wedding, and all the gardens, in the parish cut their best roses for its decoration; for this event occurred in July, the end of the rose season. Dinglefield church overflowed with roses, and the bridesmaids' dresses were trimmed with them, and every man in the place had some sort of a rosebud in his coat. And thus it was, half smothered in roses, that the young people went away.

Mr. Incledon was not heard of for years after; but quite lately he came back to Whitton married to a beautiful Italian lady, for whose sake it was, originally, as Rumor whispered, that he had remained unmarried so long. This lady had married and forsaken him nearly twenty years before, and had become a widow about the time that he left England. I hope, therefore, that though Rose's sweet youth and freshness had attracted him to her, and though he had regarded her with deep tenderness, hoping perhaps for a new, subdued, yet happy life through her means, there had been little passion in him to make his wound bitter after the mortification of the moment. The contessa was a woman of his own age, who had been beautiful, and was magnificent, a regal kind of creature, at home amid all the luxuries which his wealth provided, and filling a very different position from anything that could have been attainable by Rose. They dazzle the people on the Green when they are at Whitton, and the contessa is as gracious and more inaccessible than any queen. She smiles at them all benignly, and thinks them an odd sort of gentle savages, talking over their heads in a voice which is louder and rounder than suits with English notions. And it is reported generally that Mr. Incledon and his foreign wife are "not happy." I cannot say anything about this, one way or another, but I am sure that the happiness he shares with the contessa must be something of a very different character from that which he would have had with Rose; higher, perhaps, as mere love (you all say) is the highest; but different—and in some things, perhaps, scarcely so homely-sweet.

When Rose heard of this, which she did in the harbor of an Italian port, she was moved by interest so true and lively that her husband was almost jealous. She read her mother's letter, over and over, and could not be done talking of it. Captain Wodehouse after a while had to go on shore, and his wife sat on the deck while the blue waves grew bluer and bluer with evening under the great ship, and the Italian sky lost its bloom of sunset, and the stars came out in the magical heavens. What a lovely scene it was, the lights in the houses twinkling and rising tier on tier, the little lamps quivering at the mastheads, the stars in the sky. Rose shut her soft eyes, which were wet,—was it with dew?—and saw before her not the superb Genoa and the charmed Italian night, but the little Green with its sunburnt grass and the houses standing round, in each one of which friendly eyes were shining. She saw the green old drawing-room of the White House, and the look he cast upon her as he turned and went away. That was the day when the great happiness of her life came upon her; and yet she had lost something, she could not tell what, when Mr. Incledon went away. And now he was married, and to his old love, some one who had gone before herself in his heart, and came after her, and was its true owner. Rose shed a few tears quite silently in the soft night, which did not betray her. Her heart contracted for a moment with a strange pang—was she jealous of this unknown woman? "God bless him!" she said to herself, with a little outburst of emotion. Did not she owe him all she had in the world? good right had Rose to bid "God bless him!" nevertheless there was an undisclosed shade of feeling which was not joy in his happiness, lingering in her heart.

"Do you think we could find out who this contessa is?" she said to her husband, when he returned. "I hope she is a good woman, and will make him happy."

"Yes," said Captain Wodehouse, "he is a good fellow, and deserves to be happy; and now you can be comfortable, my dear, for you see he has consoled himself," he added, with a laugh.

www.ingramcontent.com/pod-product-compliance
Lightning Source LLC
LaVergne TN
LVHW011704200225
804198LV00008B/397